Bibliotheca Indo-Buddhica Series
Sunil Gupta, *Editor*

Bibliotheca Indo-Buddhica Series No. 126

VĀDANYĀYA OF DHARMAKĪRTI

The Logic of Debate

Critically edited and translated
with Introduction and Notes
by
Pradeep P. Gokhale

Sri Satguru Publications
A Division of
Indian Books Centre
Delhi, India

Published by :
Sri Satguru Publications
Indological and Oriental Publishers
A Division of
Indian Books Centre
40/5, Shakti Nagar,
Delhi-110007
(INDIA)

First Edition: Delhi, 1993

ISBN 81-7030-380-X

PRINTED IN INDIA

Preface

I am happy to present a translation of Dharmakīrti's *Vādanyāya* before the students and readers of Indology and Indian philosophy. When I read the text for the purpose of translation, I found that the text is still in need of critical edition because it contains some corrupt readings. So I have edited the text in the light of the editions of Rahul Sankrityayan and of Dvarikadas Shastri and also in the light of Śāntarakṣita's commentary *Vipañcitārthā*.

In my translation of the text I have tried to be neither too literal nor too liberal. The former, because I wanted to make Dharmakīrti's *Vādanyāya* intelligible to those English readers who do not understand Sanskrit. And the latter, because I wanted to be useful to those who would like to read the text with the help of a translation. I have also included explanatory notes at the end of this work in order to facilitate a clearer understanding of the text and the translation.

The central theme of *Vādanyāya* is the nature and classification of *nigrahasthānas*. I had written on this topic in the context of Nyāya and Buddhist theories of inference and fallacies, as a small part of my Ph.D. dissertation. Around the same time my colleague Dr. Mangala Chinchore had taken up the theme as the central topic of her Ph. D.

dissertation. (Co-indicidently both the dissertations have been published in the Bibliotheca Indo-Buddhica series of Indian Books Centre). Dr. Chinchore has discussed the theme with a great length and depth in her work. But while reading her work I found that my approach to *Vādanyāya* is basically different from her approach. In my Introduction to this work, therefore, I took an opportunity to express my approach as clearly as possible and also to discuss one of the crucial points made by Dr. Chinchore in her book. Thanks to Dr. Chinchore's writing which provoked me to do so.

I am grateful to Shri Sunil Gupta who asked me to translate *Vādanyāya* for Indian Books Centre and encouraged me from time to time. I am also grateful to my parents, wife, colleagues and friends who gave me encouragement and moral support when it was needed.

Pradeep P. Gokhale

November 15, 1992

Contents

Abbreviations

D	Dvarikadạs Shastri's edition of *Vādanyāya.*
(D)	Reading accepted in D.
Lit.	Literally
NBh	*Nyāyabhāṣya* of Vātsyāyana
NS	*Nyāyasūtra* of Gautama
NV	*Nyāyavārtika* of Udyotakara
R	Rahul Sankrityayan's edition of *Vādanyāya*
(R)	Reading accepted in R
V	*Vipañcitārthā,* the Śāntarakṣita's commentary of *Vādanyāya* as included in D.
(V)	Reading of *Vādanyāya* as accepted in V.
VN	*Vādanyāya* as included in this work.

Introduction

Vādanyāya is an important work by Dharmakīrti, the Buddhist philosopher and logician of seventh century A.D.. The work is devoted to the rules of victory and defeat in debate. The term '*Vādanyāya*' means the logic of debate in the broad sense of the term 'logic'. 'Logic' in its restricted sense means a formal discipline which systematises the rules governing validity of valid arguments or logical truth of the logically true propositions. But logic in its broad sense could mean a discipline which deals with the questions of rightness and wrongness from a rational point of view (that is, where 'right' stands for rational or reasonable and 'wrong' stands for irrational or unreasonable) in the context of any given enquiry. When, for instance, a debate takes place between two persons it is a legitimate question as to whose stand in the debate is rational and whose irrational. Winning and losing in a debate would be governed by the consideration of rightness or wrongness in this sense, if one has to look at 'debate' as a rational enterprise. Naturally the discipline which deals with the rules governing rationality of winning or losing a debate could be called the logic of debate. *Vādanyāya* is a work in the logic of debate in this broad sense.

The concept of nigrahasthāna

Dharmakīrti's construction of the logic of debate can be better understood on the background of Nyāya discussion of debate. Dharmakīrti has used the Nyāya account of debate, not only as a *pūrvapakṣa*, a position to be refuted, but also, at least partly, as a raw material for reconstruction. His criticism of Nyāya is not purely destructive but it has a constructive aspect also. Gautama in his *Nyāyasūtra* (hereafter, *NS*) states the rules regarding winning and losing a debate in terms of the notion of *nigrahasthāna*. Gautama presents the notion of *nigrahasthāna* ('the point of defeat') in his work in two places. First he gives the general concept of *nigrahasthāna* as *vipratipatti* and *apratipatti* (Misapprehension and non-apprehension) in *NS* 1.2.19 and in the latter part of his work he gives an elaborate classification of *nigrahasthānas*. Dharmakīrti seems to develop over the general concept of *nigrahasthāna* given in *NS*. His line of approach could be spelt out as follows: Dharmakīrti suggested that *nigrahasthānas* of the disputant (*Vādin*) and those of the opponent (*prativādin*) are not the same. The job of the disputant (as disputant) is to present a good argument for proving his position and to justify it, whereas the job of the opponent as opponent is to point out the faults in the argument. They would be failing in their jobs it they suffer from non-apprehension or false apprehension relevant to their respective jobs. The non-apprehension that the disputant has consists in his failure to present or justify a sound argument and the false apprehension he has consists in his presentation of fallacious arguments or irrelevant or redundant statements. All these types seem to be clubbed by Dharmakīrti into one term - '*asādhanāṅgavacana*'. Similarly the non-apprehension that the opponent has consists in his inability to find out the genuine fault in the faulty argument advanced by the disputant. The false apprehension he has consists in his pointing out a non-fault as fault. Both these types seem to be clubbed by Dharmakīrti in one term - '*adoṣodbhāvana*'. In this way it is possible to argue that Dharmakīrti's account of *nigrahasthāna* is not radically opposed to the Nyāya definition of *nigrahasthāna* but it is a development over it. That is why, it seems, Dharmakīrti does not criticise the general definition of *nigrahasthāna* though he criticises other aspects of the Nyāya account of *nigrahasthāna*. Two such aspects come to the foreground-

(1) The Nyāya conception of debate in the context of which the question of *nigrahasthānas* becomes relevant.

(2) The elaborate classification of *nigrahasthāna* given in *NS*.

Dharmakīrti on the Nyāya-concept of debate

Dharmakīrti's account of the nature of debate differs significantly from the Nyāya account. The first point of difference is that of terminology. What Naiyāyikas call *Vāda* is not the same as what Dharmakīrti calls *Vāda*. Naiyāyikas classify *kathā* (discussion) into three kinds: *vāda, jalpa* and *vitaṇḍā*. '*Vāda*' roughly stands for a friendly discussion between a teacher and his disciple or between two co-disciples where the question of victory or defeat does not arise. '*jalpa*' stands for a debate between two parties where both the parties try to justify their own positions against each other. In *jalpa* the question of victory and defeat is most relevant. '*Vitaṇḍā*' stands for a debate similar to *jalpa*, the difference being that in *Vitaṇḍā* one of the parties does not present any position of its own, but it only attempts to refute the position of the other party.

What Naiyāyikas call *vāda* resembles what Dharmakīrti calls *prapañcakathā* or *vistarakathā* (see, for instance, sections 70, 72, 73). *Prapañcakathā* is a diffuse discussion which is not governed by any rules concerning defeat or victory. But unlike *vāda* it is not restricted to the discussion between teacher and his disciple or between two co-disciples. It can take place between any two persons interested in a subject.

What Naiyāyikas call *jalpa* resembles what Dharmakīrti calls *vāda*. *Vāda* of Dharmakīrti (let us call it *vāda* (D)) is a debate between two parties trying to argue out their own cases and refute the cases of each other. The question of victory and defeat does arise in the case of *vāda* (D). But *vāda* (D) may be distinguished from *jalpa* in at least two important ways -

(1) The purpose behind *jalpa* is the protection of one's own philosophical determination ('तत्त्वाध्यवसायसंरक्षणार्थं जल्पवितण्डे . . .' *NS* 4.2.50). In fact Naiyāyikas associated their concepts of victory and defeat with this goal of self-protection. *Jalpa* and *vitaṇḍā* are the weapons to be used for defending oneself and for defeating others. The purpose behind *vāda*(D), on the other hand, is to persuade the other debater rationally, to help him achieve the knowledge of truth and to remove his misconceptions. Dharmakīrti associates his concepts of victory and defeat with this goal of *vāda* (D). (परानुग्रहाय तत्त्वख्यापनं वादिनो विजयः, भूतदोषदर्शनेन मिथ्याप्रतिपत्तिनिवर्तनं प्रतिवादिनः। - *VN*, Section 37). The other difference follows from this difference.

(2) Since *jalpa* (and also *vitaṇḍā*) is to be used as a weapon for self-defence (and for winning over others), the use of both rational as well as irrational devices in the course of debate was permitted by Naiyāyikas. On the contrary Dharmakīrti condemned the use of any irrational means (such as *chala*, a form of deceiving the other debater) in the course of debate, because for him the purpose of *vāda*(D) was not to defend one's own position by any hook or crook, but to benefit the other debater by removing his misconception and leading him to knowledge.

The third type of *kathā* viz., *vitaṇḍā* which was recommended by Naiyāyikas as a means to self-defence was disapproved totally by Dharmakīrti. (एतेनैव वितण्डा प्रत्युक्ता, अभ्युपगमाभावे विवादाभावात्। - *VN*, Section 83).

Dharmakīrti on classification of nigrahasthānas

We have seen that Dharmakīrti does not seem to be critical about the general definition of *nigrahasthāna* as given in *NS*, which he develops further. But he is vehemently critical about the elaborate Nyāya classification of *nigrahasthānas.* He devotes the second half of his work to the criticism of this classification. He gives his own classification of *nigrahasthānas* along with their definitions, in the first half of his work. Let us first consider his own classification and then turn to his criticism of the Nyāya classification.

Prima facie it appears that Dharmakīrti's classification of *nigrahasthānas* is just two-fold. But the two types of *nigrahasthānas* that Dharmakīrti mentions (viz. *asādhanāṅgavacana* and *adoṣodbhāvana*) in fact indicate many more types because Dharmakīrti himself derives and interprets the two terms in various ways. By interpeting the terms variously Dharmakīrti himself makes room for five kinds of *asādhanāṅgavacana* and two kinds of *adoṣodbhāvana.* His classification may be tabulated as follows-

Nigrahasthāna

Of the disputant (*Asādhanāṅgavacana*)	Of the opponent (*Adoṣodbhāvana*)
(N_1) Non-justification of a constituent of proof	(N_6) Not pointing out a fault in disputant's argument
(N_2) Non-statement of a constituent of proof	(N_7) Pointing out a non-fault as fault.
(N_3) Statement of what is redundant as a part of proof	
(N_4) Statement of a fallacious constituent of proof	
(N_5) Statement of something irrelevant	

[For the types N_1 to N_7 based on different derivations of the terms *asādhanāṅgavacana* and *adoṣodbhāvana*, see sections 1, 30, 31, 32, 33, 36 and 38 respectively]

This amounts to a seven-fold classification. If we understand this classification, then we can understand the point in Dharmakīrti's criticism of Nyāya -classification also in a better light. Dharmakīrti is not very critical, for instance, about two Nyāya - *nigrahasthānas* - *Apratibhā* (Non-imagination) and *Hetvābhāsa* (Fallacies of probans). (Of course Dharmakīrti would differ with the Nyāya conception and classification of *hetvābhāsas* in their details, but not with the basic concept of *hetvābhāsa*). It is not surprising because Dharmakīrti has included them in his own classification in some form or the other. *Apartibhā,* takes the form of N_1, N_2 or N_6 in Dharmakīrti's classification and *Hetvābhāsas* are included in N_4. In fact Dharmakīrti in one place goes to the extent to say that the two *nigrahasthānas* viz. *Hetvābhāsa* and *Apratibhā* cover all the *nigrahasthānas.* (न पूर्वोत्तरपक्षवादिनो हेत्वाभासाप्रतिभाभ्याम् अन्यन्निग्रहस्थानं न्याय्यमस्ति, तदुभयवचनेनैव सर्वमुक्तमिति, *VN,* Section 80).

Dharmakīrti accepts the Nyāya *nigrahasthāna Punarukta* (See sections 71-73) with some qualifications and modifications. It is natural because *Punarukta* in its modified form implies N_3 of Dharmakīrti. He clearly accepts '*Arthāntara*' of Nyāya (see section 61) which implies his N_5.

In general we can say that when Dharmakīrti is critical about the Nyāya classification, he is not opposed to each and every type of *nigrahasthāna* of Nyāya. He is ready to accept those Nyāya *nigrahasthānas,* which are formally matching to his classification which is more systematic. Still he is critical about the Nyāya classification to a large extent for the following reasons-

(1) *The Nyāya classification is not mutually exclusive:* Many *nigrahasthānas* which are mentioned separately in the Nyāya

list due to minor differences, could be clubbed into a few of them. For example *Pratijñāvirodha* in its refined and corrected form could be included in Hetvābhāsa. (सर्वत्रायं प्रतिज्ञाहेत्वोर्विरोधः सम्भवन् द्वयीं दोषजातिमभिपतति विरुद्धतामसिद्धतां चेति। Section 53) *Arthāntara, Nirarthaka* and *Apārthaka* insofar as they are genuine *nigrahasthānas* are different kinds of irrelevant talks; so they could be clubbed into one. *Ananubhāṣaṇa, Ajñāna* and *Apratibhā* need not be distinguished from each other insofar as their essence is concerned. In this way there is a great scope for economy in Nyāya classification.

(2) *Nor is the Nyāya - classification collectively exhaustive:* Because, if one allows invention of new types on the basis of minor differences, then any number of types can be invented, which are not there presently in the Nyāya list. (See section 80).

(3) *Dharmakīrti is critical about the Nyāya framework of anumāna:* When Naiyāyikas were not clear about the constitutive elements of a sound probans, Dharmakīri introduced the scheme of three constitutive elements. Correspondingly he pointed out three basic fallacies of probans : *Asiddha, Viruddha* and *Anaikāntika.* This was a systematic counter-thesis to the Nyāya scheme of five *Hetvābhāsas.* Naiyāyikas talked of five elements (*avayavas*) of inferential statement. Dharmakīrti systematically criticised this view and pointed out that only two elements (the statements of *pakṣadharmatā* and *vyāpti*) are necessary and sufficient and also that the order between these two elements is of no importance.[1] Whereas the Nyāya scheme of *nigrahasthānas* presupposes the Nyāya framework of *anumāna,* Dharmakīrti's criticism of the former reflects his criticism of the latter. So *Aprāptakāla* is no more a *nigrahasthāna* because it presupposes the specific order of the elements of the inferential statement. If an inferential statement lacks *Pratijñā* or *Nigamana* then the occasion of

defeat called *Nyūna* occurs according to Nyāya. Dharmakīrti rejects this possibility because, *Pratijñā* and *Nigamana* as elements of inferential statements are redundant according to him. And if *Pratijñā* itself is not necessary in any inferential statement, then many *nigrahasthānas* such as *Pratijñāntara, Pratijñāhāni, Pratijñāsaṁnyāsa* lose their significance.

(4) *Other defects:* Apart from the above defects in the Nyāya account, there are other defects. There are many places where Naiyāyikas are incorrect or vague or confused in their account. Sometimes they present implausible cases as the instances of *nigrahasthāna.* (For instance, see section 44). They unduly extend the scope of *Pratijñavirodha* and mix up *Dṛṣṭāntavirodha* with it. They treat some of the unnecessary conventions regarding debate as the essential rules (see section 78). Dharmakīrti points out many such cases into the details of which we need not go here.

A problem: Is hetvābhāsa a nigrahasthāna?

I have pointed out that Dharmakīrti in his classification of *nigrahasthānas* includes *Hetvābhāsa* as one of the derivations of the term *asādhanāṅgavacana.* (It is N_4 in his classification tabulated above). But this view is not acceptable to all. Dr. Mangala Chinchore in her thorough-going account of *Vādanyāya* repeatedly claims that *hetvābhāsa* is not a *nigrahasthāna* according to Dharmakīrti.[2] As a matter of fact there are many statements of Dharmakīrti himself which are clearly contrary to her claim.[3] But there is one passage which apparently supports Dr. Chinchore's view.

"न हि दुष्टसाधनाभिधानेऽपि वादिनः प्रतिवादिनोऽप्रतिपादिते दोषे पराजयव्यवस्थापना युक्ता, तयोरेव परस्परसामर्थ्योपघातापेक्षया जयपराजय-व्यवस्थापनात्। केवलं हेत्वाभासात् भूतप्रतिपत्तेरभावात् अप्रतिपादकस्य जयोऽपि नास्त्येव। न हि तत्त्वचिन्तायां कश्चित् छलव्यवहारः।" (Section No. 36).

Here Dharmakīrti is pointing out that commission of a *Hetvābhāsa* by the disputant does not by itself result into his defeat. He will be defeated if the fallacy of probans has been pointed out by the opponent. Nor would it be correct to say: The commission of *Hetvābhāsa*, if it remains undiscovered by the opponent, would result in to the disputant's victory, because his position stands proved insofar as it is not disproved. The disputant does not win because due to his fallacious argument, he fails to persuade his opponent rationally (भूतप्रतिपत्तेरभावात् - Literally - there is no realisation of truth (by the opponent)).

Now the question is: If *hetvābhāsa* is an occasion of defeat according to Dharmakīrti why does the commission of *Hetvābhāsa* does not necessarily result into defeat according to him?

Dr. Chinchore's answer seems to be: Since commission of a *Hetvābhāsa* does not necessarily result into defeat, *Hetvābhāsa* must not be a *nigrahasthāna* according to him. But is this approach satisfactory?

The fact is: Where Dharmakīrti calls *Hetvābhāsa* a *nigrahasthāna*, he does so literally and vividly.[4] But the passage which apparently supports Dr. Chinchore's interpretation, does not contain the word '*nigrahasthāna*' at all. (Dr. Chinchore has apparently overlooked the direct and clear evidences unfavourable to her thesis, but tried to exploit unclear and indirect evidences apparently favourable to her.) If the two evidences are put together, we have the following picture: *Hetvābhāsa* is a *nigrahasthāna* but commission of *Hetvābhāsa* does not necessarily cause the defeat.

This is interesting. If Dharmakīrti is consistent in this, then his notion of *nigrahasthāna* is in need of further clarification. I suggest the following clarification.

Nigrahasthāna, i.e., an occasion of defeat or a ground of defeat is so called because when it is committed by a disputant or an opponent in the debate situation, it can cause the defeat (subject to its discovery by the other debater). But *nigrahasthāna* is not always the *sufficient* condition of defeat (i.e. it need not necessarily lead to one's defeat); it is possible that a *nigrahasthāna* is committed but the actual defeat does not occur.[5] *Hetvābhāsa* is a *nigrahasthāna* according to Dharmakīrti in this restricted sense. In fact this situation is not peculiar to *hetvābhāsa,* it could be generalised and applied to other *nigrahasthānas* as well. In general, one could say, it could be applied to *asādhanāṅgavacana* and *adoṣodbhāvana.* (We will consider a problem with this proposal a little later.)

Dharmakīrti in this way realises a gap between winning and losing - a situation where none of the debaters is to be declared as defeated though one of them is certainly at fault, and though a *nigrahasthāna* has been committed. Why does Dharmakīrti take this stand? He himself gives the answer-

तयोरेव परस्परसामर्थ्योपघातापेक्षया जयपराजयव्यवस्थापनात्। (Section 36)

The debater who commits a fallacy but whose fallacy remains undetected by the opponent, is not defeated, because winning and losing is determined relative to the act of surpassing each other's strength that takes place among the two debaters. That one debater loses a point or fails to score a point is insufficient. Whether the other debater scores a point by surpassing him is equally important. If the disputant commits a fallacy, he has lost a point, but if the opponent does not discover the fallacy, he is equally a loser, he will score a point over the disputant, if he points out the fallacy committed by him. Committing a *nigrahasthāna* amounts to losing a point, but it will not be translated into actual defeat unless that is complemented by the other debater by scoring a point. Here Dharmakīrti is insisting that result of a debate should not be based on a one-sided judgement, but it should always be made in the light of reciprocal or competitive character of the debate. This contention in no way affects Dharmakīrti's view that *Hetvābhāsa* is a *nigrahasthāna.*

But if the judge cannot declare the disputant as defeated in the situation described above, what else can he do? It is possible to claim that the judge may declare the disputant as the winner. Because if the judge has discovered a fault in the disputant's argument which the opponent has not, but if the judge is partial to the disputant, then he could take advantage of the situation and tell the opponent, "See, the disputant has presented an argument which you are not in a position to refute. So you have lost; the disputant has won." Dharmakīrti condemns this possibility because it would be a case of cheating the opponent on the part of the judge. And no cheating practice is in order in a philosophical enquiry. (न हि तत्त्वचिन्तायां कश्चित् छलव्यवहारः। Section 36).

This approach of Dharmakīrti is important as a response to Nyāya approach also. Naiyāyikas do not talk of any gap between occurrence of a *nigrahasthāna* and actual defeat. This sometimes may generate a paradoxical situation. Consider, for instance, the two Nyāya-*nigrahasthānas* - *Hetvābhāsa* and *Paryanuyojyopekṣaṇa.* Suppose a disputant commits a fallacy of probans and the opponent fails to discover it. Then the disputant has committed the former *nigrahasthāna* whereas the opponent has committed the latter. According to Nyāya, both will have to be declared as defeated. Dharmakīrti tries to avoid this paradox by creating a gap between occurrence of *nigrahasthāna* and declaration of defeat.

But the problem reappears in a different form in Dharmakīrti's framework also. Consider the first type of *adoṣodbhāvana* (N_6), according to which the disputant is faulty, but the opponent fails to discover the fault. This is an occasion of the opponent's defeat. But the disputant has already committed a fault (which the opponent fails to discover), so it is an occasion of disputant's defeat as well. So there is an occasion (or two occasions at the same time) of the defeat of both disputant and opponent. But none of them is to be declared as defeated! What will happen now? *Adoṣodbhāvana* cannot culminate into the actual defeat of the opponent unless this incapasity of the opponent (to discover the disputant's fault) has been pointed out by the disputant himself. (Because, an incapasity of a debater cannot by itself lead to his defeat! This is by the same token as in the case of *Hetvābhāsas*.) But if the disputant points out the opponent's incapasity to discover the disputant's own fault, then he in a way acknowledges the real fault committed by himself. In discovering opponent's incapasity he is discovering his own fault.[6] He is acknowledging *asādhanāṅgavacana* committed by himself and *adoṣodbhāvana* committed by the opponent. Again a paradoxical situation! Dharmakīrti may perhaps say: Such a situation of indecision is welcome, because occurrence of a *nigrahasthāna* does not by itself play a decisive role! But still the question is: Why did Dharmakīrti introduce *adoṣodbhāvana* of the first type (i.e.. N_6) as the occasion of the opponent's defeat, which never leads to the actual defeat of the opponent?

On the present edition of the text

The Sanskrit text of *Vādanyāya* was first edited by Rahul Sankrityayan and was published by Mahabodhi Society of Sarnath in 1936. It was further edited by Swami Dvarikadas Shastri in the light of Śāntarakṣita's commentary *Vipañcitārthā* and published by Buddha-bhāratī of Varanasi in 1972. This latter edition is certainly an improvement over Rahulji's version and is closer to the original text. Yet it contains many corrupt readings and leaves room for further improvement.[7] The present edition is an attempted improvement over Dvarikadas Shastri's edition of *Vādanyāya*.

While editing, I have considered Dvarikadas Shastri's edition (hereafter, D) as the point of departure. Generally, I have accepted the alternative readings suggested in D in the light of *Vipañcitārthā* (hereafter, V). But in some places I found that the readings in Rahul Sanskrityayan's edition (hereafter, R) are more consistent than the readings in D. Generally, I have benefited from V while improving upon D. However, since V is not a word to word commentary and leaves many words and sentences unmentioned and unexplained, it cannot come to our rescue while improving upon many corrupt readings in the available text. I have suggested alternative readings in some such cases, considering mainly the question of semantic consistency of the text.

Since D is my starting point, I have given editorial footnotes only where I had to deviate from D. When the alternative readings suggested by me are based on R or V, I have altered the text accordingly and explained the source in the footnotes. But when the source of alternative reading is not R or V, but my imagination, I have introduced my suggestions in the text by placing them into brackets, and have prefixed or suffixed a question mark to them.

The main drawback of my version of *Vādanyāya* is that it, like R and D, does not take into account any Tibetan version of the text. My humble request to the scholars of Tibetan would be to verify the alternative readings suggested by me in the light of Tibetan versions of *Vādanyāya*. In spite of this drawback, I would like to claim humbly that my version is closer than R or D to the original, though it still contains many doubtful places.

Lastly I would like to inform that the division of the text (and the translation) into sections and the assignment of section-numbers has been done by me for the convenience of the readers. These sections or section numbers are not there in the original text.

Notes and References

1. For Dharmakīrti's framework of *anumāna* and the way it differs from Nyāya framework, see Chapters II, III and V of *Inference and Fallacies Discussed in Ancient Indian Logic* by Pradeep P. Gokhale, Sri Satguru Publications (Indian Books Centre), Delhi, 1992.

2. Dr. Mangala Chinchore makes this claim vividly on pp. 83-84 of her work *Vādanyāya: A Glimpse of Nyāya-Buddhist controversy* (Sri Satguru Publications, Indian Books Centre, Delhi, 1988) Elsewhere in her work she makes the point in different form such as - "*Nigrahasthānatva* and *Hetvābhāsatva* should not be confused with each other. None of the two determines the other." She attributes this view to Dharmakīrti. But I think that, that *Hetvābhāsatva* is a determiner of *Nigrahasthānatva* would be acceptable to Dharmakīrti if that amounts to saying that commission of *Hetvābhāsa* is a *nigrahasthāna* because it is what it is. This is so because commission of *Hetvābhāsa* is nothing but *asādhanāṅgavacana* in one of the senses of the latter (See section 32) and *asādhanāṅgavacanatva* is definitely a determiner of nigrahasthānatva.

3. (i) 'अथवा साधनस्य सिद्धेर्यत् नाङ्गम् असिद्धः विरुद्धः अनैकान्तिको वा हेत्वाभासः, तस्यापि वचनं वादिनो निग्रहस्थानम् असमर्थोपादानात्' *(VN*, Sec. 32).

   (ii) 'न पूर्वोत्तरपक्षवादिनो हेत्वाभासाप्रतिभाभ्याम् अन्यन्निग्रहस्थानं न्याय्यमस्ति तदुभयवचनेनैव सर्वमुक्तमिति' (*VN*, Sec. 80).

   (iii) 'हेत्वाभासाश्च यथान्यायं निग्रहस्थानमिति, एतावन्मात्रमिष्टमिति' (*VN*, Sec. 92).

4. See Note 3 above.

5. Dr. Chinchore observes that the Nyāya concept of *Nigrahasthāna* was different from Dharmakīrti's concept. she points out that Udyotakara uses the term *Parājayavastu* (the point of defeat) where as Dharmakīrti uses the term *Parājayādhikaraṇa* (the ground of defeat). This is an important observation indeed. But Dr. Chinchore does not use it while considering the question whether *Hetvābhāsa* is a ***nigrahasthāna.*** She could have said: *Hetvābhāsa* is a ***nigrahasthāna*** in Dharmakīrti's sense. It is a ground of defeat, which may or may not result into actual defeat. But it is not a *nigrahasthāna* in Naiyāyikas' sense. It is not of point of defeat (*Parājayavastu*) which indicates actual defeat.

6. This situation is similar to *Matānujñā* in Nyāya terms.

7. Prof. Hajime Nakamura, in his foreword to *वादन्याय: वाद प्रक्रिया का तार्किक विश्लेषण (गौतमीय एवं बौद्धन्याय के संदर्भ में)*, a Hindi work by Prof. Ramachandra Pandeya, Dr. Raghavendra Pandeya and Dr. Manju, congratulates the authors of the work for editing the Sanskrit text of *Vādanyāya* successfully. But the Sanskrit text which the authors include in their work as its second appendix is nothing but a word to word (and error to error) reproduction of Dvarikadas Shastri's edition (with the deletion of his editorial footnotes, but without the deletion of footnote numbers in the text). The authors do not care to acknowledge Svami Dvarikadas Shastri anywhere in the work.

वादन्यायः
VĀDANYĀYA

Part I

निग्रहस्थानलक्षणम्

Definition of 'Occasion of Defeat'[1]

१. न्यायवादिनमपि वादेषु असद्व्यवस्थोपन्यासैः शठा निगृह्णन्ति, तन्निषेधार्थमिदमारभ्यते।

असाधनाङ्गवचनमदोषोद्भावनं द्वयोः।
निग्रहस्थानम् , अन्यत्तु न युक्तमिति नेष्यते॥

इष्टस्यार्थस्य सिद्धिः साधनम्, तस्य निर्वर्तकम् अङ्गम्, तस्य अवचनं तस्याङ्गस्यानुच्चारणं वादिनो निग्रहाधिकरणम्; तदभ्युपगम्य अप्रतिभया तूष्णीम्भावात्। साधनाङ्गस्यासमर्थनाद् वा।

1. The wicked persons defeat in debates by employing improper methods[2] (Lit. Systems) even the one who argues rationally. We start this (work on the logic of debate) for repudiating them.

Asādhanāṅgavacana and *adoṣodbhāvana*[3] are the occasions of defeat of the two (debaters, i.e. the disputant and the opponent respectively). Any other occasion of defeat, however, is not just; hence we do not accept it.

Sādhana means proof of the matter[4] intended (to be proved by the disputant). Its *aṅga* means what constitutes it. Its non-statement, i.e. non-utterance of that constituent (of proof), is the occasion of defeat of the disputant; (this occurs) either because the disputant keeps mum because of Non-imagination after he proposes (to prove the matter) or because he does not justify the constituent of proof (which he states).[5]

† § †

२. [स्वभावहेतौ साधनाङ्गसमर्थनम्][१]

त्रिविधमेव हि लिङ्गमप्रत्यक्षस्य सिद्धेरङ्गम् - स्वभाव:, कार्यम्, अनुपलम्भश्च।

तस्य समर्थनं साध्येन व्याप्तिं प्रसाध्य धर्मिणि भावसाधनम्। यथा 'यत् सत् कृतकं वा, तत् सर्वमनित्यम्, यथा घटादि:, सन् कृतको वा शब्द:' इति।

2. **[Justification of the constituent of proof in the case of self-nature as reason.]**

Because, three kinds of inferential sign (= probans) constitute the proof of an unperceived object: self-nature, effect and non-apprehension. Its justification (i.e. justification of probans) means nothing but proving its existence in the property-bearer (= subject of the thesis), after proving its pervasion with the probandum (= predicate of the thesis). For example - "All that is real or is a product is impermanent, like the things such as pot. And sound is real or a product."

† § †

३. अत्रापि न कश्चित् क्रमनियम:, इष्टार्थसिद्धेरुभयत्राविशेषात् ।

यस्माद् धर्मिणि प्राक् सत्त्वं प्रसाध्य पश्चादपि व्याप्ति: प्रसाध्यत एव। यथा - 'सन् शब्द: कृतको वा, यश्चैवं स सर्वोऽनित्य:, यथा - घटादि:' इति।

---

१. This and other subtitles given in brackets have been introduced first in D. They are not in R.

3. In this there is no rule about the order (of premises)[1] because the two cases make no difference as to the establishment of the intended matter. Because, pervasion can certainly be demonstrated afterwards, after proving the existence (of the probans) in the property-bearer. For example - "Sound is real or a product. And whatever is of this kind is all impermanent, like the things such as pot." (This also is a legitimate proof).

† § †

४. अत्र व्याप्तिसाधनं विपर्यये बाधकप्रमाणोपदर्शनम्।

यदि न सर्वं सत् कृतकं वा प्रतिक्षणविनाशि स्याद्, अक्षणिकस्य क्रमयौगपद्याभ्यामर्थक्रियाऽयोगाद् अर्थक्रियासामर्थ्यलक्षणमतो व्यावृत्तम् - इत्यसदेव स्यात्।

सर्वसामर्थ्योपाख्याविरहलक्षणं हि निरुपाख्यमिति।

एवं साधनस्य साध्यविपर्यये बाधकप्रमाणानुपदर्शने विरोधाभावादस्य विपर्ययवृत्तेरदर्शने सन् कृतको वा स्यात्, नित्यश्च इत्यनिवृत्तिरेव शङ्कायाः।

4. Here proving pervasion means demonstrating an evidence[1] (= *pramāṇa*) which falsifies (the existence of probans) where there is absence (of probandum).[2] (It is as follows.) If all that is real or a product is not subject to destruction at every moment, then the defining characteristic (of the real) viz. 'capacity to function' gets excluded from it. Because a non-momentary object cannot have any function (= *artha-kriyā*) either in succession or in simultaneity. Hence it (= the non-monetary object) will be unreal. Because the entity, which by definition is destitute of all the descriptions in term of capacity,[3] is indescribable (as real etc.).

If the evidence which falsifies the existence of probans in the absence of probandum, is not shown in this way, it (=

the possibility that probans may exist in the absence of probandum) is not contradicted (by any means of knowledge). And hence when it (= probans) is not seen to exist in the absence (of probandum), there is no suspension of the doubt that the sound may be real or a product and yet permanent.

† § †

५. न च सर्वानुपलब्धिर्भावस्य बाधिका, तत्र सामर्थ्यं क्रमाक्रमयोगेन व्याप्तं सिद्धम्; प्रकारान्तराभावात्।

तेन व्यापकधर्मानुपलब्धिरक्षणिके सामर्थ्यं बाधते।

क्रमयौगपद्यायोगस्य सामर्थ्याभावेन व्याप्तिसिद्धेर्नानवस्थाप्रसङ्गः।

5. Not every (kind of) non-apprehension falsifies the existence of an object. In the given case capasity of an object is established as pervaded by 'the association with succession or lack of succession', because there is no other mode. Therefore (in this case) the non-apprehension of pervading characteristic (viz. 'succession or no succession') falsifies the capasity in the case of the non-momentary object.[1] Because the pervasion of the 'non-association with succession or simultaneity' with the absence of capacity is proved, there is no occurrence of infinite regress.[2]

† § †

६. अत्राप्यदर्शनमप्रमाणम्, यतः क्रमयौगपद्यायोगस्यैवासामर्थ्येन व्याप्त्यसिद्धेः पूर्वकस्यापि हेतोरव्याप्तिः। इहापि पुनः साधनोपगमेऽनवस्थाप्रसङ्ग इति चेत्। न; अभावसाधनस्यादर्शनस्याप्रतिषेधात्।

यददर्शनं विपर्ययं साधयति हेतोः साध्यविपर्यये, तदस्य विरुद्धप्रत्युपस्थानाद् बाधकं प्रमाणमुच्यते।

एवं हि स हेतुः साध्याभावेऽसन् सिध्येत्, यदि तत्र प्रमाणवता स्वविरुद्धेन बाध्येत। अन्यथा तत्रास्य बाधकासिद्धौ संशयो दुर्निवारः।

ततो व्यतिरेकस्य सन्देहादनैकान्तिकः स्याद्धेत्वाभासः।

नाप्यदर्शनमात्राद् व्यावृत्तिः; विप्रकृष्टेष्वसर्वदर्शिनोऽदर्शनस्याभावासाधनाद्, अर्वाग्दर्शनेन सतामपि केषाञ्चिदर्थानामदर्शनात्।

6. **[An Objection-]**

"But here non-apprehension is not the means to knowledge because the pervasion of the non-association with succession or simultaneity with the absence of capasity is itself not proved.[1] Hence there is no pervasion of the earlier probans ('realness') (with the probandum 'momentariness'). If you proceed to accept (another) probans for (proving) this (second pervasion), then there will be the danger of infinite regress."

[Answer] That is not correct. Because you have not denied (successfully) the non-apprehension as the means to prove absence.

(Which kind of non-apprehension is called the falsifying evidence in this case?) That non-apprehension, which proves the absence of probans in the case in which there is absence of probandum, is called the falsifying evidence because it establishes the opposite of that (= existence of probans in the absence of probandum).

In this way the probans will be proved as absent from the case in which probandum is absent, if it (= its existence) is falsified by the authoritative contrary evidence. Otherwise if the evidence falsifying it (= the existence of probans) in that (= the absence of probandum) is not established, then the doubt (that the probans may exist without probandum) is inevitable.

In that case there will be a fallacy of probans called 'Inconclusive' because of the doubtfulness of negative concomitance.

Nor is the exclusion (of probans from the case of the absence of probandum) proved merely on the basis of non-apprehension. Because in the case of remote objects non-apprehension does not prove their absence to a non-omniscient being; and because a person with downword vision[2] does not perceive some objects although they are real.

† § †

७. बाधकं पुनः प्रमाणम्। यत्र क्रमयौगपद्यायोगो न तस्य क्वचित् सामर्थ्यम्। अस्ति चाक्षणिके स इति प्रवर्तमानमसामर्थ्यमसल्लक्षणमाकर्षति। तेन 'यत् सत् कृतकं वा तदनित्यमेव' इति सिध्यति।

तावता साधनधर्ममात्रान्वयः साध्यधर्मस्य स्वभावहेतुलक्षणं च सिद्धं भवति।

एवं स्वभावहेतुप्रयोगेषु समर्थितं साधनाङ्गं भवति। तस्यासमर्थनं साधनाङ्गावचनम्। तद् वादिनः पराजयस्थानम्; प्रारब्धार्थासाधनात्। वस्तुतः समर्थस्य हेतोरुपादानेऽपि सामर्थ्याप्रतिपादनात्।

7. The falsifying evidence, however, is (expressed as follows)[1]: Anything which lacks association with succession and simultaneity does not have capacity to do anything. And the non-momentary object has this character (that it lacks association with succession and simultaneity). The falsifying evidence which goes onwards in this way entails (Lit. attracts) 'the absence of capacity' which is the defining

characteristic of 'unreal'. By that (the pervasion-) 'what is real or a product is definitely impermanent' is proved.

By this (justification) the positive concomitance of the whole[2] probans-characteristic with the probandum-characteristic is proved.

In this way the constituent of proof becomes justified in the arguments based on self-nature as reason. Not justifying it is non-statement of a constituent of proof. It is an occasion of defeat of the disputant because it amounts to non-fulfilment of the purpose undertaken (by the disputant). Because, the soundness of the reason has not been brought out (by the disputant), there, although in fact a sound reason has been employed.

† § †

८. [**कार्यहेतौ साधनाङ्गसमर्थनम्**]

कार्यहेतावपि **साधनाङ्गस्य** समर्थनम्। यत् कार्यं लिङ्गं कारणस्य साधनायोपादीयते, **तस्य तेन सह** कार्यकारणभावप्रसाधनं भावाभावप्रसाधन-प्रमाणाभ्याम्। **यथा** - '**इदमस्मिन्** सति भवति', 'सत्स्वपि तदन्येषु समर्थेषु तद्धेतुषु तदभावे न **भवति**' इति।

एवं ह्यस्यासन्दिग्धं तत्कार्यत्वं समर्थितं भवति। अन्यथा केवलं 'तदभावे न भवति' इत्युपदर्शने अन्यस्यापि तत्राभावे सन्दिग्धमस्य सामर्थ्यम्। अन्यत् तत्र समर्थं, तदभावात् तत्र भूतम्।

एतन्निवृत्तौ पुनर्निवृत्तिर्यदृच्छासंवादः। मातृविवाहो हि तद्देशजन्मनः पिण्डखर्जूरस्य देशान्तरेषु मातृविवाहाभावेऽभाववत्। एवं हि समर्थितं तत् कार्यं सिध्यति।

सिद्धं तत् स्वसम्भवेन तत्सम्भवं साधयति, कार्यस्य कारणाव्यभिचारात्।

अव्यभिचारे च स्वकारणैः सर्वकार्याणां सदृशो न्यायः।

एवमसमर्थनं कार्यहेतावपि साधनाङ्गावचनं तद् वादिनः पराजयस्थानम्। असमर्थिते तस्मिन् कार्यत्वासिद्धेरर्थान्तरस्य तद्भावाप्रतिबद्धस्वभावस्य भावे तद्भावनियमाभावात्, आरब्धार्थासिद्धेर्वस्तुतः कार्यस्याप्युपादाने तदप्रदिपादनात्।

8. **[Justification of the constituent of proof in the case of effect as reason.]**

In the case of effect-as-reason too, a constituent of proof needs justification. (The nature of this justification is as follows:) It is the establishment of cause-effect-relation (between probans and probandum) where the effect is used as probans for proving the cause. This is done by giving two kinds of evidences (= *pramāṇas*), one establishing existence (i.e. positive concomitance) and the other non-existence (i.e. negative concomitance) such as 'This (= smoke etc.) occurs (only) when this (= fire etc.) exists' and 'In spite of the presence of other powerful causal conditions,[1] this (= smoke etc.) does not occur in the absence of this (= fire etc.)'.

In this way the fact that this (= smoke etc.) is the effect of this cause (= fire etc.) (and not of any other thing) becomes justified indubitally. Otherwise if (while establishing the negative concomitance) only this much is demonstrated, that 'This does not occur in the absence of this,' then the (causal) efficacy of it (= of the alleged cause) will be doubted, if other things are also absent there (when the effect is absent). The doubt will be as follows: 'Some other thing is efficient in producing it (= the effect), and it (= the effect) did not occur because of the absence of that (other thing)'.[2]

'Absence of this while that is absent' amounts to accidental coincidence. For example the fact that marriage with one's own mother is granted in a particular place is related with the generation of date-trees in that place and the fact that there is absence of date-trees in other places where marriage with one's own mother is not granted, is a matter of mere coincidence. Thus the effect is proved if justified properly.

When any real thing is proved, it proves the generation of its cause through its own generation. Because the effect has invariable relation with the cause. There is the common law (of causation) in so far as the invariable relation of all effects with their causes is concerned.

(Like in the case of self-nature as reason:) In the case of effect as reason too, not justifying (the casue-effect-relation) in this way is 'non-statement of a constituent of proof' and is the occasion of the disputant's defeat.

Because when it (= the cause-effect-relation) is not justified, the proposed thesis remains unproved, because the effect-hood of the effect is unproved, as there is no rule by which something (Lit. that) exists when some other object which has no binding relation with it, exists; because although effect (as reason) is employed as a matter of fact, its effecthood is not proved.

† § †

९. [अनुपलब्धावपि साधनाङ्गसमर्थनम्]

अनुपलब्धावपि प्रतिपत्तुरुपलब्धिलक्षणप्राप्तस्यानुपलब्धिसाधनं समर्थनम्; 'तादृश्या एवानुपलब्धे'[1] रसद्व्यवहारसिद्धेः। अनुपलब्धिलक्षणप्राप्तस्य प्रतिपत्तृप्रत्यक्षोपलब्धिनिवृत्तावप्यभावासिद्धेः।

तत्रोपलब्धिलक्षणप्राप्तिः स्वभावविशेषः कारणान्तरसाकल्यं च। स्वभावविशेषो यन्न त्रिविधेन विप्रकर्षेण विप्रकृष्टम्। यदनात्मरूपप्रतिभासविवेकेन प्रतिपत्तृप्रत्यक्षप्रतिभासरूपम्। तादृशः सत्स्वन्येषूपलम्भप्रत्ययेषु तथाऽनुपलब्धोऽसद्व्यवहारविषयः, अन्यथा सति लिङ्गे संशयः।

१. (V): तादृशस्यात्र चानुपलब्धे - (R): तादृश्या एव चानुपलब्धे - (D)

9. **[The justification of a constituent of proof in the case of non-apprehension (as reason)]**

In the case on non-apprehension (as reason) too, (justification of a constituent of proof means) proving non-apprehension of the object fulfilling the condition of 'apprehensibility'[1] by the knower.[2] Because it is only by this kind of non-apprehension that the practice of non-existence[3] is proved.

If the object does not fulfil the condition of apprehensibility, then its absence is not proved even if it is not apprehended perceptually by the knower.

Here 'fulfilling the condition of apprehensibility' means (1) the specific nature (of the object) and (2) the aggregate of all the remaining conditions (of apprehension). The specific nature of the object means that the object is not remote (from senses) due to (any of the) three kinds of remoteness.[4] It is the nature which appears in the perceptual appearance to the knower, in contradistinction with the appearance of something other than self-nature. When the object is not apprehended in spite of the presence of other conditions of the apprehension of such an object, the non-apprehended object is the object of the practice of non-existence. Otherwise there arises a doubt (about non-existence) in spite of (non-apprehension as) the reason.

† § †

१०. अत्रापि सर्वमेवंविधमसद्व्यवहारविषय इति व्याप्तिः, कस्यचिदसतोऽभ्युपगमे तल्लक्षणाविशेषात्।

न ह्येवंविधस्यासत्त्वानभ्युपगमेऽन्यत्र तस्य योगः। न ह्येवंविधस्य सतः सत्स्वन्येषूपलम्भकारणेष्वनुपलब्धिः। अनुपलभ्यमानं त्वीदृशं नास्तीत्येतावन्मात्रनिमित्तोऽयमसद्व्यवहारः, अन्यस्य तन्निमित्तस्याभावात्।

10. The pervasion here is of the form, "Everything of this kind is the object of the practice of non-existence; because (for instance) the same characteristic (viz. non-apprehension associated with fulfilment of the condition of apprehensibility) commonly exists in the accepted case of some non-existent object."

Because unless non-existence of the object of this kind is accepted, non-existence will not be obtainable in other cases. Because if the object of this kind exists and the other conditions of apprehension are present,, then there will not be non-apprehension. If on the other hand the object of this kind is not apprehended, then it does not exist. This much is the (sufficient) condition of the practice of non-existence, because there is no other condition.

† § †

११. सर्वसामर्थ्यविवेको निमित्तमिति चेत्। एवमेतत्, तस्यैव सर्वसामर्थ्यविवेकिन एवं प्रतीतिः, अन्यस्य तत्प्रतिपत्त्युपायस्याभावात्। तत्प्रतिपत्तौ च सत्यामसद्व्यवहार इतीदं तन्निमित्तमुच्यते।

11. **A possible objection:**

"Exclusion of all capasities (from the object) is the condition (of non-existence)"

[Answer] That is right. But the experience of the non-existent object, which (as, you say,) excludes all capasities, takes place in this way (i.e. in the way explained by us), because there is no other means to its experience. And when the non-existent object is experienced in this way, it is practised as non-existent. That is why we call this as its condition.

† § †

१२. बुद्धिव्यपदेशार्थक्रियाभ्यः सद्व्यवहारो विपर्यये चासद्व्यवहार इति चेत्। भवति बुद्धेर्यथोक्तप्रतिभासायाः सद्व्यवहारः, विपर्ययेऽसद्व्यवहारः।

प्रत्यक्षाविषये तु स्याल्लिङ्गजाया अपि कुतश्चित् सद्व्यवहारः।

असद्व्यवहारस्तु तद्विपर्ययेऽनैकान्तिकः, विप्रकृष्टेऽर्थे प्रतिपत्तृप्रत्यक्षस्य अन्यस्य वा प्रमाणस्य निवृत्तावपि संशयात्।

12. **A possible objection:** "The practice of existence (of an object) originates from cognition, verbal usage and pragmatic function (of the object) whereas the practice of non-existence originates from the absence of them."

[Answer] (Yes) The practice of existence originates from the cognition, the appearance of which takes place as has been stated above.[1] And the practice of non-existence originates from its opposite. But when the object is not the object of perception, the practice of existence could originate from an inferential cognition.

But the practice of non-existence is uncertain (= inconclusive) in the case of absence of it (= perceptual cognition) (i.e. in the case of non-perceptual object). Because in the case of a remote object although the knower's perception or some other means to knowledge becomes inoperative, the doubt (that the object may be existent), remains.

† § †

१३. न च सर्वे बुद्धिव्यपदेशास्तद्भेदाभेदौ वा वस्तुसत्तां वस्तुभेदाभेदसत्तां वा साधयन्ति, असत्स्वपि कथञ्चिदतीतानागतादिषु नानैकार्थक्रियाकारिषु वाऽर्थेषु तद्भावख्यापनाय नानैकात्मताऽभावेऽपि नानैकरूपाणां वृत्तेः – राजा महासम्मतः

प्रभवो राजवंशस्य, शङ्खश्चक्रवर्ती महासम्मतनिर्मितस्य यूपस्योत्थापयिता, शशविषाणं, [२]रूपं[२] सनिदर्शनं सप्रतिघं, घटश्चेति।

13. It is also not the case that all cognitions and linguistic usages or the distinctions or identities amongst them prove the existence of things or the existence of distinctions or identities amongst the things. Because there are cognitions and linguistic usages to indicate the existence of objects which are non-existent somehow, because they belong either to past or future or the objects which have multiple or singular functions; (similarly) there are (cognitions or linguistic usages with) multiple or singular form, although the objects (indicated by them) lack multiplicity or singularity (respectively). (For example) - (i) (Past object-) The king Mahāsammata, the originator of the monastry. (ii) (Future object-) The emperor Śaṅkha would elevate the sacrificial post established by Mahāsammata. (iii) (Unreal object-) The horn of a hare (iv) (Singular object with multiple functions-) colour that is perceptual and restrictive (v) (composite object with a singular function-) Pot.[1]

† § †

१४. नहि सनिदर्शनादिशब्दा नानावस्तुविषयाः, एकत्रोपसंहारात्।

नानाविषयत्वेऽप्येकत्रोपसंहारस्तन्निमित्तानां तत्तत्समवायादिति चेत्। आयासे बतायं तपस्वी पदार्थे [पदार्थः?] पतितोऽनेकसम्बन्धिनमुपकृत्यानेकं शब्दमात्मनि तेभ्यः समाशंसन्! स यैः [३]शक्तिभेदैरनेकसम्बन्धिन[३] मुपकरोति, तैरेवानेकं शब्दं किं नोत्थापयति! एवं ह्यनेन परम्परानुसारपरिश्रमः परिहतो भवति।

---

२. (V); कथं - (R) and (D).

३. (V): शक्तिभेदैरनेकं सम्बन्धिन - (R) and (D).

नानाशब्दोत्थापनासामर्थ्ये नानासम्बन्ध्युपकारोऽपि मा भूत्, अनुपकारे हि तेषां तत्सम्बन्धिताऽपि न सिध्यति। घट इत्यपि च रूपादय एव बहव एकार्थक्रियाकारिण एकशब्दवाच्या भवन्तु, किमर्थान्तरकल्पनया?

बहवोऽपि हि एकार्थकारिणो भवेयुः, चक्षुरादिवत्। तत्सामर्थ्यख्यापनाय तत्रैकशब्दनियोगोऽपि स्यादिति युक्तं पश्यामः।

14. In this the words like 'perceptual' ('*sanidarśana*') (which are used for describing colour) do not designate many objects because they consolidate in one object.

[A possible objection by Vaiśesikas:] "Many descriptions, although they correspond to many objects, consolidate in one object because the objects causing them (= those descriptions) are related by Inherence (*samavāya*) with the respective (single) object."

[Answer] The poor fellow object (such as colour-object) has fallen into a burdensome task, because it directs many words from many related factors towards itself, when it favours a multi-termed relation (called Inherence)[1]! Why does not the object (colour) stimulate different words, with respect to the same different capasities, through which it favours the multi-terned relation (called Inherence)? By this the strain of following (endless) series[2] can be avoided by it (= by the object such as colour).

If (according to you, the Vaiśeṣika,)[3] one and the same object cannot stimulate different words, then let it not favour the multi-termed relation as well. And if it does not favour it, then it (= the object) cannot be proved to be related with them (= many terms of the relation). Similarly many entities such as colour etc. which have one (collective) pragmatic function may be named by a singular word namely 'pot'. What is the use of imagining a different entity (pot, over and above colour etc.)? Many entities can have one pragmatic function, like (the entities such as) eye etc. (which have perceptual cognition as their collective function). So we think it proper that a single word may be applied to many entities to indicate the single capasity (that they have).

† § †

१५. न च निष्प्रयोजना लोकस्यार्थेषु शब्दयोजना। तत्र येऽर्थाः सह पृथग्वा एकप्रयोजनाः तेषां तद्भावख्यापनाय हि एकशब्दो नियुज्येत यदि, किं स्यात्? तदर्थक्रियाशक्तिख्यापनाय नियुक्तस्य समुदायशब्दस्यैकवचनविरोधोऽपि नास्त्येव; सहितानां सा शक्तिरेका, न प्रत्येकमिति।

समुदायशब्द एकस्मिन् समुदाये वाच्ये एकवचनं घट इति।

जातिशब्देष्वर्थानां प्रत्येकं सहितानां च शक्तिर्नानैका च शक्तिरिति, नानैकशक्तिविवक्षायां बहुवचनमेकवचनं चेच्छातः, वृक्षा वृक्षमिति [? वृक्ष इति] स्यात्।

यद्येष नियमो बहुष्वेव बहुवचनम् एकस्मिन्नेकवचनमिति।

अस्माकं तु साङ्केतिकेष्वर्थेषु सङ्केतवशात् ˣतावित्यˣ भिनिवेश एव।

15. Moreover, people do not apply words for objects without any purpose. What will be the harm if for many objects which serve a single purpose either collectively or distributively, a single word is used for indicating that the objects are like that (i.e. that they serve common purpose)? Similarly there is no contradiction in using a group-word (for many entities) in singular, when it is used for indicating

ˣ Suggested in R; तैरित्य - mentioned in R; ताप्य - (D); Grammatically त इत्य - (= ते इत्य -) would be correct.

their common pragmatic function, because they have that single efficacy collectively and not distributively.

So the group-word is used in singular, when it denotes a single group of objects, as the word 'pot'.

But in the case of class-words, the objects (belonging to the same class) may have single (common) capasity either individually or collectively or they may have many different capasities or the same capasity. Hence the class-word can be used either in plural or in singular, according to one's desire, if one intends to talk of many capasities or one capasity (respectively). For example one may use the word 'trees' or 'tree' (according to one's intention).

While (according to you) it is the rule that plural form is used only when objects are many (i.e. more than two in number) and singular form is used when the object is one, our view is that the two (kinds of words) are used by convention in their conventional senses. So it (= what you are saying) is only an (undue) adherence (on your part).

† § †

१६. नानेको रूपादिरेकशब्दोत्थापने समर्थ इति चेत्। किं वै पुरुषवृत्तेरनपेक्षाः शब्दानर्थाः स्वयमुत्थापयन्ति, आहोस्वित् पुरुषैः शब्दा व्यवहारार्थमर्थेषु नियुज्यन्ते? स्वयमुत्थापने हि भावशक्तिः, अशक्तिर्वा चिन्त्येत। न च तद्युक्तम्, पुरुषैस्तेषां नियोगे यथेष्टं नियुञ्जीरन्निति कस्तत्रोपालम्भः?

निमित्तं च नियोगस्योक्तमेव।

अपि च – यदि न रूपादीनामेकेन शब्देन सम्बन्धः, 'कथमेकेनैषा[५]-माश्रयाभिमतेन द्रव्येण सम्बन्ध इति केवलमयमसद्भूताभिनिवेश एव।

५. (R); कथमनेकेषा - (D).

न वयमेकसम्बन्धविरोधादेकं शब्दं नेच्छामः, अपि त्वभिन्नानां रूपादीनां घटकम्बलादिषु नानार्थक्रियाशब्दविरोधात् ते एकरूपाः 'समुदायान्तरा'[६]-सम्भाविनीमर्थक्रियामेव न कुर्युः; तेन तत्प्रकाशनायैकेनापि शब्देनोच्येरन्।

भवतु नाम कस्यचिदियं वाञ्छा - 'भवेयुरेकरूपा रूपादयः सर्वसमुदायेषु' इति। किमिदं परस्परविविक्तरूपप्रतिभासाध्यक्षदर्शनमेनामुपेक्षते?

अनिष्टं चेदं रूपादीनां प्रतिसमुदायं स्वभावभेदोपगमात्।

16. **[A possible objection by Vaisesikas:]**

"(The characteristics of the pot viz.) colour etc., which are plural in number cannot stimulate a single word."

[Answer:] Do the objects themselves stimulate the words irrespective of the intention of the person (i.e. the speaker) or it is the persons who use the words for objects, in order to conduct practises? Because the question whether the objects have real capasity or no capasity can be thought about only if objects themselves give rise (to words). But this (position) is not reasonable. Then what is your censure, when you say that if the words are applied by persons, then they will be applied by them at will (i.e. without any rule)?

We have already told the efficient cause of the application of words.

Moreover, if colour etc. (being many) do not have relation with a single word, then how can they (= colour etc.) have any relation with the single substance which is regarded as the substratum of them?[1] Therefore this is nothing but the ghost of falsehood[2] possessing you.

---

६. (V); समुदायोत्तरा - (R) and (D).

[The Opponent Vaiśeṣika says:] "We do not intend to say that one word should not be used for many objects as they are opposed to any relation with a single object. But we say that colour etc., when they are non-different (i.e. one and the same) in pots, blankets etc., are opposed to differential pragmatic functions and to (the use of) different words. Hence when they (= colour etc.) are one and the same in nature, they will not have the pragmatic function which other collections of objects cannot have.[3] Therefore, in order to indicate it (i.e. the sameness of colour in spite of diversity of collections which share it) the colour etc. can be mentioned by a single word."[4]

[Answer:] One could have an inclination to say, "colour etc. would be the same through all the collections." (here we ask) Does the perceptual knowledge of the mutually distinct appearances of colour set aside this inclination?[5] Moreover, this view (of our opponents) is not desirable because colour etc. are accepted to be different in nature from one collection to another.

† § †

१७. यद्यन्य एव रूपादिभ्यो [७]घट: स्यात् किं[७] स्यात्?

अस्तु, तस्य प्रत्यक्षस्य सतोऽरूपादिरूपस्य तद्विवेकेन बुद्धौ स्वरूपेण प्रतिभासने किमावरणम्?

प्रतिभासमानाश्च विवेकेन [८]प्रत्यक्षार्था[८] दृश्यन्तेऽपृथग्देशत्वेऽपि गन्धरसादय:, वातातपस्पर्शादयश्चैकेन्द्रियग्राह्यत्वेऽपि।

---

७. (V); घटादीनामेक: - (R) and (D).

८. (R); प्रत्यक्षा अर्था - (D).

इदमेव च प्रत्यक्षस्य प्रत्यक्षत्वं यदनात्मरूपादिविवेकेन स्वरूपस्य बुद्धौ समर्पणम्। अयं पुनर्घटादिरमूल्यदानक्रयी यः स्वरूपं च नोपदर्शयति, प्रत्यक्षतां च स्वीकर्तुमिच्छति।

17. **[The opponent asks:]** "What (wrong) will happen if pot would be distinct from colour etc.?"

[Answer] All right. What then is the obstacle[1] that obstructs the appearance of the real perceptible thing (like pot), which is not of the form of colour etc., in its own form distinct from them (= colour etc.), in our cognition?[2]

The perceptible objects such as odour and taste are seen to appear distinctly even when they do not have separate location (i.e. even when they belong to the same thing). And the objects such as the touch of the wind and the touch of sun's heat are seen to appear distinctly even if they are sensible by the same sense organ.[3]

This is what makes perception a perception, namely, the submission of object's own nature, as distinct from the nature of what it is not, to the cognition. But this thing such as pot (as conceived by you) is a free-of-cost-purchaser,[4] who does not exhibit its own (distinct) nature, but wants to appropriate (distinct) perceptibility.

† § †

१८. एतेन बुद्धिशब्दादयोऽपि व्याख्याताः, यदि तैस्तत्साधनमिष्यते।
न च प्रत्यक्षस्यानभिभवे रूपानुपलक्षणम्; येन तत्साधनाय लिङ्गमुच्यते।
अप्रत्यक्षत्वेऽप्यप्रमाणस्य सत्तोपगमो न युक्तः। तत्र रूपादिभ्योऽन्यो घटः
एवं तावन्न बुद्धिव्यपदेशाभ्यां सत्ताव्यवहारः, सत्ताभेदाभेदव्यवहारो वा।

अत एव न तद्विपर्ययाद् विपर्ययः।

18. This (= above explanation) also explains the (distinct) cognition, the (distinct) word (i.e. verbal usage) etc., if it desired (by the opponent) to prove it (= distinct existence of the pot etc.) on the basis of them.[1]

Moreover, it is not correct to say that the colour is not identified (distinctly) when the perception (of the composite object such as pot) is not dominated (by some other object), in which case (i.e. only if the colour is not identified distinctly,) a probans will be stated for proving it (= the distinct composite object such as pot).[2]

When it (= the composite object) is not perceptible, it is not proper to assert the existence of a thing, for the knowledge of which there is no authoritative means. Therefore pot is not different from colour etc.

In this way one cannot talk of existence just on the basis of cognition and verbal usage, nor can one talk of distinctness or identity of existence (on the basis of them).

For the same reason the obsence cannot be established on the basis of the absence of them (= cognition, verbal usage etc.).[3]

† § †

१९. अर्थक्रियातस्तु सत्ताव्यवहारः स्यात्, न सत्ताभेदाभेदव्यवहारः, एकस्याप्यनेकार्थक्रियादर्शनात्। यथा प्रदीपस्य विज्ञानवर्तिविकारज्वालान्तरोत्पादनानि। अनेकस्यापि चक्षुरादेरेकविज्ञानक्रियादर्शनात्।

न ब्रूमः - अर्थक्रियाभेदमात्रेण सत्ताभेद इति। किं तर्हि? अदृष्टार्थक्रियाभेदेन। या अर्थक्रिया यस्मिन्नदृष्टा पुनर्दृश्यते, सा सत्ताभेदं साधयति। यथा मृद्यदृष्टा सत्युदकधारणाद्यर्थक्रिया घटे दृश्यमाना। अदृष्टा च तन्तुषु प्रावरणाद्यर्थक्रिया पटे दृश्यते इति सत्ताभेदः।

सिध्यत्येवमर्थान्तरं, तथाऽप्यवयवी न सिध्यति। यथाप्रत्ययं संस्कारसन्ततौ [१]स्वभावभेदो[१]त्पत्तेरर्थक्रियाभेदः। अरणिनिर्मथनावस्थादाविवाग्नेः स्थूलकरीष-तृणकाष्ठदहनशक्तिभेदः, तथा यथाप्रत्ययं स्वभावभेदोत्पत्तेस्तन्त्वा-दिष्वर्थक्रियाभेदः।

एतेन बुद्धिव्यपदेशभेदाभेदौ व्याख्यातौ।

19. One can talk of existence on the basis of pragmatic function, but one cannot talk of distinctness or identity of existences on the basis of it. Because a single object is seen to have many pragmatic functions. For example a lamp has the following functions: (helping) cognition, transformation of the wick and producing another flame. (Distinctness or identity of existences cannot be established on the basis of pragmatic functions.) Because, (for example) although eye and the other (causal) factors are many in number, they are seen to have a single function viz. (perceptual) cognition.

[The opponent says:] "We are not saying that distinctness of existences is established merely on the basis of distinctness of pragmatic functions. But (it can be so established) on the basis of distinctness of some unseen pragmatic function. The pragmatic function which is not seen in one thing (at one point of time) but is seen there again, establishes distinctness of existence. For example the function of carrying water which is not seen in mud is seen in the earthen pot and the function of covering body which is not seen in threads is seen in the cloth. In this way there is the distinctness of existences."

[Answer:] In this way (the existence of) some other object may be established, but the composite whole (= *ayayavī*) is not establihsed. The difference in

---

१. (V): स्वभेदो - (R) and (D).

pragmatic function (in the cases cited by you) is due to the difference of nature (= *svabhāva*) which occurs in a series of modifications in accordance with its causal conditions.[1] For example, when the fire is in the stage of rubbing of the fire-producing sticks, the pragmatic function of fire differs due to whether it is produced in thick cow-dung or in grass or in wood. In the same way different pragmatic function can be found in threads etc. because the nature of a thing differs in accordance with the difference in causal conditions.

This explains the distinctness and identity of cognitions and verbal usages (as the alleged evidences of distinctness and identity of existences).[2]

† § †

२०. तत्र यदुक्तम् -' अर्थक्रियात: सत्ताव्यवहारसिद्धि:, विपर्ययाद् विपर्यय:' इति; सत्यमेतत्। स एव तु विपर्ययोऽनुपलब्धिलक्षणप्राप्तेषु न सिध्यति।

तत्र पुनरिदमनिच्छतोऽप्यायातम् - 'यस्येदं सामर्थ्यमुपलब्धिलक्षणप्राप्तं सन्नोपलभ्यते, सोऽसद्व्यवहारविषय:, सामर्थ्यलक्षणत्वात् सत्त्वस्य' इति।

तथापि कोऽतिशय: पूर्वकादस्य? न हि स्वभावादर्थान्तरं सामर्थ्यम्। तस्योपलब्धिलक्षणप्राप्तस्य योऽनुपलम्भ: स स्वभावस्यैवेति पूर्वकैवेयमनुपलब्धि:।

तस्मादनेन क्वचित् केषाञ्चिदसद्व्यवहारमभ्युपगच्छता अतोऽनुपलम्भादभ्युपगन्तव्य:।

सोऽन्यत्रापि तथाविधेऽविशिष्ट इति सोऽपि तथास्तु इति। न वा क्वचिद्, विशेषाभावात्। व्याप्ति: - सर्व एवंविधोऽनुपलब्धोऽसद्व्यवहारविषय इति।

20. [**Objection**:] "But it has been said (by you yourself) that the (linguistic) practice of existence is proved on the basis of pragmatic function and its (i.e. former's) absence is proved on the basis of its (i.e. latter's) absence."

[**Answer**:] That is right. But that absence is not proved in the case of those objects which do not fulfil the condition of apprehensibility.

So one has to accept even against one's will: 'That is the object of the practice of non-existence, the capasity of which fulfils the condition of apprehensibility and yet is not apprehended. Because capasity is the mark of existence.'

But what does this statement score over the earlier one? Because, capasity is not a different object from self-nature. So the non-apprehension of the capasity fulfilling the condition of apprehensibility is nothing but the non-apprehension of the self-nature of the object. So this non-apprehension is the same as the earlier one.[1]

Therefore the one who accepts the practice of non-existence of something in some place, should accept it on the basis of this (kind of) non-apprehension.

This (non-apprehension) is common to other similar cases.[2] So let them be like that (i.e. let the other cases be equally the cases of non-existence). Or let it be (i.e. let non-existence be proved) in no case, because there is no difference (amongst these cases insofar as non-apprehension is concerned). The pervasion (here is as follows): Every thing which is of this kind (i.e. which fulfils the condition of apprehensibility) and is not apprehended is the object of the practice of 'non-existence.'[3]

† § †

२१. नैव कश्चित् क्वचित् कथञ्चिदनुपलब्धोऽप्यसद्व्यवहारविषय इति चेत्। सर्वस्य सर्वरूपाणां सर्वदाऽनिवृत्तेः सर्वं सर्वत्र सर्वदा समुपयुज्येत।

इदं च न स्यात् - 'इदमतः', 'नात इदम्', 'इहेदम्', 'इह नेदम्', 'इदानीमिदम्', 'इदानीं नेदम्', 'इदमेवम्', 'इदं नैवम्' इति; कस्यचिदपि रूपस्य कथञ्चित् क्वचित् कदाचिद् विविक्तहेतोरभावात्। अनन्वयव्यतिरेकं विश्वं स्यात्, भेदाभावात्।

अवस्थानिवृत्तिप्रवृत्तिभेदेभ्यो व्यवस्थेति चेत्। नन्वत एव सर्वविषयस्यासद्-व्यवहारस्याभावान्न ते सम्भवन्ति, यतस्तेभ्यो व्यवस्था स्यात्।

क्वचिद् विषयेऽसद्व्यवहारोपगमे स कुत इति वक्तव्यम्। न ह्यनुपलम्भा-दन्यो व्यवच्छेदहेतुरस्ति; विधिप्रतिषेधाभ्यां व्यवच्छेदे सर्वदाऽनुपलम्भस्यैव साधनत्वात्।

अनुपलम्भादेव तदभ्युपगमे, स यत्रैवास्ति सर्वोऽसद्व्यवहारविषय इति वक्तव्यम्, विशेषाभावात्।

21. **[A possible objection by a Sāṅkhya opponent[1]]** "Nothing is an object of the practice of 'non-existence' whatever it may be and wherever and in whatever way it may remain non-apprehended."

[Answer:] In that case everything will be applicable everywhere all the time, because every form of everything will remain incessant all the time.

Moreover, the following (situations) will not occur - 'This (is) out of this;' 'This (is) not out of this;' 'This (is) here'; 'This (is) not here'; 'This (exists) now'; 'This (does) not (exist) now'; 'This (is) of this kind'; 'This (is) not of this kind'. Because there will not be any distinct cause of any (particular) form of an object in any way, anywhere, any time. The universe will be without co-existences and co-absences because there will not be any distinction.

[**A possible objection**:] "There will be order (in the universe) on the basis of the distinctions between disappearance and appearance of states (= *avasthā*) (of things)".

[**Answer**:] These distinctions themselves are not possible in your system on the basis of which there will be order; because the practice of non-existence of anything is untenable (according to you).[2]

If you accept the linguistic practice of non-existence in the case of some objects, then you will have to tell how that is tenable. Because there is no probans proving non-existence except non-apprehension. When non-existence is proved either on the basis of positive evidences or negative evidences[3], non-apprehension is always the probans.

If one accepts the thesis that it (= the practice of non-existence) is on the basis of non-apprehension only, then one has to say that everything is the object of the practice of non-existence, wherever that (= non-apprehension) is there. Because there is no difference among these cases (in so far as they are the cases of non-apprehension).

† § †

२२. सर्वप्रमाणनिवृत्तिरनुपलब्धिः। सा यत्र सोऽसद्विषय [? सोऽसद्व्यवहार-विषय] इष्ट इति चेत्। सुकुमारप्रज्ञो देवानांप्रियो न सहते 'प्रमाणचिन्ता'[1]-परिक्लेशं, येन नात्रादरं कृतवान्!

न ह्यनुमानादिनिवृत्तिरभावं गमयति, व्यभिचारात्। न सर्वप्रत्यक्षनिवृत्तिः, असिद्धेः।

नात्मप्रत्यक्षाविशेषनिवृत्तिरपि विप्रकृष्टेषु।

तस्मात् स्वभावविशेषो यतः प्रमाणान्नियमेन सद्व्यवहारं प्रतिपद्यते, तन्निवृत्तिस्तस्यासद्व्यवहारं साधयति, तत्स्वभावसत्तायाः तत्प्रमाणसत्तया इष्टेः।

न चोपलब्धिलक्षणप्राप्तस्यार्थस्याप्रत्यक्षादन्योपलब्धिः, येनानुमानादस्योपलब्धिः स्यात्। न च तद्रूपान्यथाभावमन्तरेणाप्रत्यक्षता, अन्यथाभावे च तदेव न स्यात्।

अपि च - कुत इदममन्त्रौषधमिन्द्रजालं भावेन शिक्षितम्, यदयमजातानष्टरूपातिशयोऽव्यवधानदूरस्थानस्तस्यैव 'तदवस्थेन्द्रियादेरेव'[2] पुरुषस्य कदाचित् प्रत्यक्षः, अप्रत्यक्षश्च; येन कदाचिदस्यानुमानमुपलब्धिः, कदाचित् प्रत्यक्षं, कदाचिदागमः! 'एकस्मिन्नेवानतिशये'[3] अमीषां प्रकाराणां विरोधात्।

22. **[Another opponent says:]** "Non-apprehension means cessation (i.e. inapplicability) of all the means of knowledge. We regard something as an object of the practice of non-existence if it is not apprehended in this sense."

[Answer :] Oh! You the beloved of gods have so delicate intelligence that you cannot tolerate the exertion of thinking about means of knowledge. That is why you did not pay serious attention to it.

---

१. (V): प्रमाणचिन्ताव्यवहार - (R) and (D).

२. (V): तदवस्थेन्द्रियादेरिव - (R) and (D).

३. (V): तस्मान्नैवानतिशये - (R) and (D).

Because, the cessation of inference etc. does not lead us to the knowledge of absence because there is variability of relation (= *vyabhicāra*) (between, say, non-inferability and absence).[1] Nor does 'the cessation of perception by all (beings)' lead us to the knowledge of absence, because that (= the cessation of perception by all beings) is unproved.[2]

Even the absolute (= *aviśeṣa*) cessation of the perception by oneself cannot (lead to the knowledge of the absence of objects), when the objects are remote.

Therefore the cessation of only that means of knowledge can prove the practice of non-existence (of an object), on the basis of which the specific nature of the object is invariably called existent. Because the existence of the (specific) nature is expected to be proved by the existence of the (specific) means to knowledge.[3]

Nor is it the case that if the object which reaches the condition of apprehensibility is not perceived,[4] then its apprehension will be of different nature (i.e. other than perception), in the case of which its apprehension could be through inference! Nor can an object (which is there and perceptible) remain unperceived, unless the nature of the object has undergone transformation. But in the case of transformation the object will not remain the same.

Moreover, wherefrom has the fellow (i.e. the Sāṅkhya opponent) learnt this magic-without-chanting-and-medicine? Because (according to the Sāṅkhya opponent) the same object is sometimes the object of perception, sometimes not, in which case its apprehension is sometimes the same as inference; sometimes it is perception, sometimes knowledge by verbal testimony! And this happens even though no excess in the nature of objet is generated or destroyed; the object is not either concealed or remote and the person (= the observer) is the same with the sense-organs etc. in the same condition as before!

Because when the object is one and the same without any excess, these characteristics (viz. sometimes perceptible, sometimes not perceptible, but inferable etc.) are incompatible.

† § †

२३. नानतिशयनिवृत्त्या, [नैकातिशयनिवृत्त्या?][१] अपरातिशयोत्पत्त्या च तैर्व्यवहारभेदोपगमात्।

सोऽतिशयस्तस्यात्मभूतोऽनन्वये [... नन्वय:?][२] निवर्तमान: प्रवर्तमानश्च कथं न स्वभावनानात्वमाकर्षयति, सुखदु:खवत्। सान्वयत्वे च का कस्य प्रवृत्तिर्निवृत्तिर्वा इति यत्किञ्चिदेतत्।

अथवा यदि च कस्यचित्स्वभावस्य प्रवृत्तिर्निवृत्तिर्वेति स्वयमप्यभ्यनुज्ञायते, तदेतदेव परो ब्रुवाण: किमिति नानुमन्यते?

तस्य निरन्वयोपजननविनाशोपगमादिति चेत्।

कोऽयमन्वयो नाम? भावस्य जन्मविनाशयो: शक्ति:; साऽस्त्येव प्रागपि जन्मनो निरोधादप्यूर्ध्वम्। तेनायं नापूर्व: सर्वथा जायते, न पूर्वो विनश्यतीति।

यदि सा सर्वदाऽनतिशया, किमिदानीमतिशयवद् यत्कृतोऽयं व्यवहार-विभाग:?

---

१. This is how the interpretation in V goes.

२. अनन्वय इत्येकान्तेन निवर्तमान:। - Interpretation in V ... नवयवे (R).

ता अवस्था अतिशयवत्य इति चेत्, ता अवस्थाः सा च शक्तिः किमेको भावः? आहोस्वित् नाना?

एकश्चेत् कथमिदानीमिदमेकत्राविभक्तात्मनि निष्पर्यायं परस्परव्याहतं योक्ष्यते - जन्माजन्म, निवृत्तिरनिवृत्तिः, एकत्वं नानात्वं, प्रत्यक्षताऽप्रत्यक्षता, अर्थक्रियोपयोगः अनुपयोगश्चेत्यादि।

23. **[Another opponent says:]** "The object is not without an excess. Because the objects assume different (linguistic) practices (such as the practice of existence and the practice of non-existence) on account of cessation of one excess and generation of another."[1]

[Answer:] If the excess in the object is identical with the object itself, and it ceases to exist and comes into existence without continuity,[2] then how does it not entail diversity in the nature of the object? - For example pleasure and pain (lack continuity and are diverse in nature).

On the other hand if the thing has continuity, then what is (its) generation or cessation and what is it the generation or cessation of? So this (= your argument) is insignificant.

Or if you yourself accept generation or cessation of a certain self-nature (of the object), then why donot you approve of the same thing when it is stated by your opponent?

[The Sāṅkhya opponent may say:] "That is because he (= our opponent, i.e. the Buddhist) accepts generation and destruction destitute of any continuity."

[The author asks:] What is this 'continuity' (= *anvaya*)?

[Opponent answers:] "It is the capasity of a thing to get generated and destroyed. It exists even before the generation and after the destruction.

Therefore this (= 'continuity' or 'continuous capasity') is not such that it did not exist before but gets generated all the way or it existed before but gets destroyed."

[The author asks:] If that capasity does not undergo any change (Lit. excess) at any time, then what does undergo the change due to which there is the distinction between the (linguistic) practices?[3]

[The opponent may say:] "It is the states (= *avasthā*) (and not the capasities) that undergo change."

[The author asks:] Are the states and the capasity one and the same thing, or are they different?

[The opponent may answer:] "One and the same thing."

[The author asks:] Now, how can you apply mutually contradictory predicates such as generation, destruction; cessation, non-cessation; oneness, manyness; perceptibility, imperceptibility; having pragmatic function and not having it, to one and the same uniform object, without relativising them to different modalities (= *niṣparyāyam*)?

† § †

२४. अस्ति पर्यायोऽवस्था शक्तिरिति, तेनाविरोध इति चेत्। विस्मरणशीलो देवानाम्प्रियः प्रकरणं न लक्षयति। शक्तिरवस्थेत्येको भावोऽविभाग इति यत् कोऽयं विरोध उक्तः?

अथाप्यनयोर्विभागः, न कश्चिद् विरोधः, केवलं सान्वयौ भावस्य जन्मविनाशौ इति न स्यात्।

तस्माद् यस्यान्वयो न तस्य जन्मविनाशौ, यस्य 'च'[1] तौ न तस्यान्वयः।

१. (R); वा – (V) and (D).

तयोरभेदाददोष इति चेद्, अनुत्तरं बत दोषसङ्कटमत्रभवान् दृष्टिरागेण प्रवेश्यमानोऽपि नात्मानं चेतयति। अभेदो हि नामैक्यम्, 'तौ' इत्ययं च भेदाधिष्ठानो भाविको व्यवहारः। निवृत्तिप्रादुर्भावयोः अनिवृत्तिप्रादुर्भावौ, स्थितावस्थितिः इत्यादिकं नानात्वलक्षणं च कथं योत्स्यते?

अथ हि भावानां भेद एतद्विरहश्चाभेदः, यथा - सुखादिषु शक्त्यवस्थयोश्चै-कात्मनि। अन्यथा भेदाभेदलक्षणाभावाद् भेदाभेदयोरव्यवस्था स्यात्सर्वत्र।

तदात्मनि प्रादुर्भावोऽभेदः, विपर्यये भेदः, यथा - मृदात्मनि प्रादुर्भवतो घटस्य तस्मादभेदः, भेदश्च विपर्यये सुखदुःखयोरिति इदं भेदाभेदलक्षणं, तेनाविरोध इति चेत्।

न वै मृदात्मनि घटस्य प्रादुर्भावः। किं तर्हि? मृदात्मैव कश्चिद् घटः, न ह्येकस्त्रैलोक्ये मृदात्मा। प्रतिविज्ञप्तिप्रतिभासभेदश्च द्रव्यस्वभावभेदात्। एवं ह्यस्यापि सुखादिषु चैतन्येषु भेदावगमः समर्थो भवति।

यद्येवं, भेदः स्यात्।

सत्यप्येतस्मिन् कस्यचिदात्मनोऽन्वया [२]देवमिति[२] चेत्। सुखादिष्वप्ययं प्रसङ्गः, चैतन्येषु च।

न च घटादिष्वपि सर्वात्मनाऽन्वयः, अवैश्वरूप्यसहोत्पत्त्यादिप्रसङ्गात्।

न च घटं मृदात्मानं च कश्चिद् विवेकेनोपलक्षयति, येनैवं [३]स्यादिदमिह[३] प्रादुर्भूतमिति।

न ह्यधिष्ठानाधिष्ठानिनोर्विवेकेनानुपलक्षणे एवं भवति। न च शक्तेः शक्त्यात्मनि प्रादुर्भावः इति तस्याः स्वात्मनोऽभेदो न स्यात्!

24. [**The Opponent may answer**:] "There is a (considera-tion of) modality, namely state and capasity (are the two modalities).[1] Therefore there is no contradiction."

२. (R); दैक्यमिति (D).

३. (V); स्यादिति नेह - (R) and (D).

[The author says:] You, the beloved of gods, are forgetful, as you are not noticing the context. What a contradiction you have made, as you have said that capasity and state are one and the same thing without any distinction!

Even if there is a distinction between them (= state and capasity), there is no contradiction (by itself), but then it only would not be the case that generation and destruction of a thing are qualified by (its) continuity.

Therefore the thing which has continuity, does not have generation or destruction and the thing which has the latter, does not have continuity.

[The opponent may say:] "There is no fault (in our argument) because there is no difference between them."

[Answer:] The respectable fellow (i.e. the Sāṅkhya opponent) is being rushed into a crowd of faults due to his attachment to his own view; yet he is not making himself aware (of it). Because non-difference means oneness. But referring to them as 'they two' (= *tau*) is the genuine (linguistic) practice based on (their) difference. There is also the definition of manyness (difference), "If the thing lacks cessation and origination inspite of the (other thing undergoing) cessation and origination, if it lacks staticity inspite of the staticity (of the other thing) etc. (then that thing is different from the other thing.)" How is (all) this co-tenable?

[The opponent might say:] "The difference amongst things and the absence of such a difference, that is, non-differences (= *abheda*) are (exemplified) as follows - pleasure, (pain), etc. (are different from each other and) capasity and state of one and the same thing (are non-different from each other). If we don't accept this, then, due to the absence of distinctive marks of difference and non-difference, there will be disorder between difference and non-difference everywhere.

"So (we accept the distinctive marks of difference and non-difference as follows)- arising in a thing-itself is non-difference; to the contrary is difference. For example pot arises in mud-itself, so it is non-different from mud. But there is difference if the case is to the contrary; (for instance) pleasure and pain (do not arise from each other, so there is difference between them). These are the distinctive marks of difference and non-difference. Hence there is no contradiction."

[Answer:] The pot does not arise in the mud-itself. But some mud-itself is called pot. Because the nature (= *ātmā*) of mud is not the same everywhere in the universe. The difference between reflective cognitions (*prativijñapti*) (of a thing) and between appearances (of it) are due to the difference between the natures of things. That is how it is possible for him (= the Sāṅkhya opponent) also to know that pleasure, (pain,) etc. (are different) and consciousnesses (i.e. *pursuṣas* according to Sānkhya) are different.[2]

If that is so, then there will be difference (between pot and the whole mud etc.)

[The opponent might say:] "It (= The non-difference between pot and mud etc.) is the case inspite of this (difference), because of the continuity of some (part of the) nature."

[Answer:] The same consequence will follow in the case of pleasure etc. and also in the case of consciousnesses.

Even in the case of pot etc. there is no continuity (of mud etc.) in all respects. Because (otherwise) the following difficulties will result -

(i) *(avaiśvarūpya -)* There cannot be (the generation of) all the forms (if the whole mud has continuity with a pot only).

(ii) (*sahotpati*-) There will be simultaneous production (of different states of a thing)

- and other difficulties.

Moreover, nobody observes the pot and its mud-nature distinctly, in the case of which it would have been possible (to say:) 'this (pot) has arisen in this (mud)'.

Because, it does not become possible when the substratum and the superstratum are not observed distinctly.

Moreover, it is not the case that a capasity arises in the locus (lit. self, nature) of the capasity.[3] Therefore there will not be non-difference between capacity and its locus.

† § †

२५. एतेनैव परिणामः प्रत्युक्तः। योऽपि हि कल्पयेद् – 'यो यस्य परिणामः स तस्मादभिन्नः' इति। न हि शक्तिरात्मनः परिणाम इति।

किञ्चेदमुक्तं भवति – परिणाम इत्यवस्थितस्य द्रव्यस्य धर्मान्तरनिवृत्तिः, धर्मान्तरप्रादुर्भावश्च परिणामः।

यत्तद्धर्मान्तरं निवर्तते प्रादुर्भवति च, किं तत् तदेवावस्थितं द्रव्यं स्यात्, ततोऽर्थान्तरं वा, अन्यविकल्पाभावात्?

यदि तत्तदेव, तस्यावस्थानान्न निवृत्तिप्रादुर्भावाविति कस्य ताविति वक्तव्यम्।

अवस्थितस्य धर्मान्तरमिति च न सिध्यति। न हि तदेव तस्यानपाश्रितव्यपेक्षाभेदं धर्मान्तरं भवति।

अथ द्रव्यादर्थान्तरं धर्मः, तदा तस्य निवृत्तिप्रादुर्भावाभ्यां न द्रव्यस्य परिणतिः। न ह्यर्थान्तरगताभ्यां स्यात् निवृत्तिप्रादुर्भावाभ्यामर्थान्तरस्य परिणतिः, चैतन्येऽपि प्रसङ्गात्।

द्रव्यस्य धर्म इति च व्यपदेशो न सिध्यति, सम्बन्धाभावात्। न हि कार्यकारणभावादन्यो वस्तुसम्बन्धोऽस्ति।

न चानयोः कार्यकारणभावः, स्वयमतदात्मनोऽतत्कारणत्वात्, धर्मस्य द्रव्यादर्थान्तरभूतत्वात्।

अर्थान्तरत्वेऽपि धर्मकारणत्वे, अर्थान्तरस्य कार्यस्योत्पादनात् द्रव्यस्य परिणामः इतीष्टं स्यात्। तद्विरुद्धस्यापि हेतुफलसन्ताने मृद्द्रव्याख्ये, पूर्वकान्मृत्पिण्ड-द्रव्यात् कारणादुत्तरस्य घटद्रव्यस्य कार्यस्योत्पत्तौ 'मृद् द्रव्यं परिणतम्' इति व्यवहारस्योपगमात्।

न च धर्मस्य द्रव्यात् तत्त्वान्यत्वाभ्यामन्यो विकल्पः सम्भवति, उभयथा येन परिणामः।

25. The same (argument) answers (the doctrine of) transformation (*pariṇāma*). Because whosoever imagines 'whatever is a transformation of something is non-different from it' is like that (i.e., is liable to the above criticism). Because, the capacity of a thing is not (the same as) its transformation.

Moreover, it happens to be said (by Sāṅkhyas): "Transformation (of a substance) is cessation of some property of the subsisting substance. Transformation is also the arisal of a different property in that substance."

(Now we ask:) Is that particular property which ceases or arises, the same as the subsisting substance or it is different from it.? Because there is no other alternative.

If it (= arising or ceasing property) is the same as that (= substance), then, because the substance subsists, there will not be cessation or arisal (of any of its properties). So tell us, to whom do they (= cessation and arisal) belong?

Nor can it be proved that the subsistent thing has got another property (which arises or ceases), because the thing itself cannot be another property of itself, unless it is (attributed to the thing) depending upon a different enquiry.[1]

If (on the contrary) a property is a different object from the substance, then the cessation and arisal of that property do not constitute the transformation of the substance. Because cessation and arisal of one object cannot amount to transformation of another object. Because (by the same token), it (= transformation) will have to be accepted in the case of consciousness also.[2]

Moreover, the linguistic expression 'the property of a substance' cannot be justified because there is no relation (between substance and property). Because, there is no real relation except cause-effect-relation.

And there is no cause-effect relation between them (= substance and property), because (according to you) a thing which itself is not of the same nature as that (= effect) is not the cause of that, and because a property is a different object from a substance.

If (you say that) something could be a cause of its property even if it is different (from that), then this will amount to your admission that the substance has undergone transformation by way of producing the effect which is a different object (from that). (But this is improper). Because your opponent (= Buddhist) would also accept the linguistic practice "The mud-substance is transformed (into a pot)" regarding the cause-effect series called mud-substance when from the earlier substance namely the lump of mud, which is the cause, the later pot-substance, which is the effect, is produced.[3]

Nor is there any (third) alternative position of a property with respect to a substance apart from sameness and otherness, so that transformation would be justified in any of the two cases.[4]

† § †

२६. न निर्विवेकद्रव्यमेव धर्मः, नापि द्रव्यादर्थान्तरम्, किं तर्हि? द्रव्यस्य सन्निवेशोऽवस्थान्तरम्, यथा अङ्गुलीनां मुष्टिः। न ह्यङ्गुल्य एव निर्विवेका मुष्टिः, प्रसारितानाममुष्टित्वात्।

नाप्यर्थान्तरं, पृथक्स्वभावान्नोपलब्धिरिति चेत्। न, मुष्टेरङ्गुलिविशेषत्वात्। अङ्गुल्य एव हि काश्चन मुष्टिः, न तु सर्वाः। न हि प्रसारिता अङ्गुल्यो निर्विवेकस्वभावाः मुष्ट्यङ्गुल्यः, अवस्थाद्वयेऽपि उभयप्रतिपत्तिप्रसङ्गात्।

[४]यत्र चर्हि[४] खलु विवेकः स्वभावभूतः, स एव वस्तुभेदलक्षणं सुखदुःखवत्।

परभूते च विवेकोत्पादेऽङ्गुल्यः प्रसारिता एवोपलभ्येरन्। न हि स्वयं स्वभावादप्रच्युतस्यार्थान्तरोत्पादेऽन्यथोपलब्धि[५]रतिप्रसङ्गात्[५]।

ननूक्तं, 'द्रव्यमेव निर्विवेकमवस्था, नापि द्रव्यादर्थान्तरम्' इति।

उक्तमिदं, न पुनर्युक्तम्। न हि सतो वस्तुनस्तत्त्वान्यत्वे मुक्त्वा अन्यः प्रकारः सम्भवति, तयोर्वस्तुनि परस्पर परिहार-स्थितिलक्षणत्वेनैकत्यागस्यापरोपादाननान्तरीयकत्वात्।

अङ्गुलीषु पुनः प्रतिक्षणविनाशिनीष्वन्या एव प्रसारिताः, अन्या मुष्टिः।

तत्र मुष्ट्यादिशब्दा विशेषविषयाः, अङ्गुलीशब्दः सामान्यविषयः, [६]बीजाङ्कुरादिशब्दवत्,[६] व्रीह्यादिशब्दवच्च। तेनाङ्गुल्यः प्रसारिता न मुष्टिः।

४. (R); य एव - (V) and (D).
५. (V); रिति प्रसङ्गात् - (R) and (D).
६. (V); बीजादङ्कुरादिशब्दवत् - (D).

26. **[The Sāṅkhya opponent might object:]**

"It is not true to say that the undifferentiated[1] (= *nirviveka*) substance is itself the property. Nor is the property a different object from the substance. What is a property then? It is an arrangement of the substance, i.e., a different state of it. For example, fist of fingers (is an arrangement or a different state of fingers). The fingers themselves without differentiation do not make a fist, because (, for instance,) the spread fingers do not make a fist.

Nor is it (= a fist) a different object from that (= fingers), because it is not observed as distinct in nature."[2]

[Answer] No. Because, fist is fingers in particular form. Certain fingers are themselves a fist, but not all fingers make a fist. Because (for instance) spread fingers in undifferentiated nature are not the fingers in the form of a fist. Otherwise one will be forced to accept the experience of both (the forms of fingers) in both the states.

Because, when differentiation (i.e. the specific qualification) is the very nature of the thing, the same becomes a mark of distinction of the thing, like pleasure and pain.

If (on the other hand) the specific qualification (= viveka) (of fingers) arises as alien (from them), then the fingers will be apprehended as spread only. Because the object which does not itself deviate from its own nature, is not apprehended as different (from itself) (even) when some other object is produced, as that (= claiming that it is apprehended as different) would amount to transgression (of reason).

[The Opponent says:] "But we have said that a state (of a substance) is (neither) the substance itself without differentiation, nor an object other than the substance."[3]

[**Answer**:] You have said this but what you have said is not correct. Because there is no (third) possibility apart from thatness and otherness in the case of any real thing. Because thatness and otherness stay in a real object by excluding each other essentially. Therefore abandoning one of them is invariably concomitant with accepting the other.

And fingers being subject to destruction every moment, the spread fingers are different and the fist is different.

Here the words like 'fist' have the particulars as their objects; the word 'fingers' has the universal as its object. For example the words like seed, sprout (apply to the particular states of rice) and the words like rice (are general terms). Therefore the spread fingers are not the same as the fist.

† § †

२७. तद्यदि प्रागसदेव कारणे कार्यं भवेत्, किं न सर्वः सर्वस्मात् भवति, न ह्यसत्त्वे कश्चिद् विशेष इति?

ननु सर्वत्र सत्त्वेऽप्ययं तुल्यो दोषः – न हि सत्त्वे कश्चिद् विशेषः, विशेषे वा [७]स विशेष[७] स्त्रैगुण्याद् भिन्नः स्यात्, [८]तद्भावे[८] विशेषस्यानन्वयात्।

सतश्च सर्वात्मना निःस्वभावावस्थायामिव किं जायते? साधनवैफल्यं च, साध्यस्य कस्यचिदभावात्।

यस्य कस्यचिदतिशयस्य तत्र कथञ्चिदसत उत्पत्तौ सोऽतिशयस्तत्र असन् कथं जायेत? जातो वा सर्वः सर्वस्माज्जायेत इति तुल्यः पर्यनुयोगः।

नातिशयस्तत्र सर्वथा नास्ति, कथञ्चित्सत एव भावादिति चेत्। यथा नास्ति स प्रकारः, तत्र अमन् कथं जायेत?

७. (V); सद्विशेष - (R) and (D).

८. (V); तदभावे - (R) and (D).

27. **[The opponent asks:]** "So if the effect is not pre-existent in the cause, why is not everything produced from everything? Because there is no difference (between various cases) in so far as (previous) non-existence (of the effect) is concerned."

[Answer] Even if (one concedes that) the effect has (previous) existence in all the cases (of causation), the same fault is there. Because there would be no difference (between various cases) in so far as (previous) existence (of the effect) is concerned.[1] and if there is difference (between different cases because anything cannot be produced from everything) then that real difference (i.e., the specific characteristic of an effect) will be distinct from the three strands (= *guṇas*, of *prakṛti*). Because in spite of the existence of them (= the three stands of *prakṛti*) (in all the effects), the specific characteristic of an effect does not extend (to other cases).

And what is produced from a thing which is existent in absolute sense of the term (= *sarvātmanā*), like something which is in the accomplished state?[2] Moreover, (if the effect is pre-existent in the cause,) the means (to the production of the effect) will be futile, because (according to you) there is nothing to be brought about.

[The opponent might say:] "Some special characteristic (Lit., excess) which was non-existent there somehow, could. be produced."

[Answer] How could that special characteristic which was not existent there, be produced? And if it could be produced, then every-thing (which was non-existent) could be produced from everything.

The objection is common (to your position and mine).

[**The opponent might say:**] "The special characteristic is not totally absent, because something can come into existence only if it is (already) existent in some form."

[**Answer**] (Though existent in some form, the characteristic was non-existent in some other form. Now the question is:) How can the characteristic be produced in the form in which it was non-existent?

† § †

२८. न च सर्वथा सतः कश्चिज्जन्मार्थ इत्युक्तम्। असतोऽपि कार्यस्य कारणादुत्पादे यो यज्जननस्वभावस्तत एव तस्य जन्म, नान्यस्मादिति नियमः।

तस्यापि स स्वभावनियमः स्वहेतोरित्यनादिस्वभावनियमः।

अपि च - यदि मृत्पिण्डे घटोऽस्ति, कथं तदवस्थायां न पश्चाद्वदुपलब्धिः, तदर्थक्रिया वा?

व्यक्तेरप्रादुर्भावादिति चेत्। तस्या एव तदर्थक्रियादिभावे घटत्वात् तद्रूपस्य च प्रागसत्त्वात् कथं घटोऽस्ति? न हि रूपान्तरस्य सत्त्वे रूपान्तरमस्ति।

न च रूपप्रतिभासभेदे वस्त्वभेदो युक्तः, अतिप्रसङ्गात्।

28. We have said hat if a thing exists in absolute sense of the term (= *sarvathā*) then there is no point in its generation. Even in the case of the production of the non-existent effect, there is a law that the effect is produced only from that thing which has a natural tendency to produce that effect, not from any other thing.

Again that causal factor is produced only from its own cause and not anything else. This is the law of nature. In this way the (causal) law of nature is beginningless.

Moreover, if the pot exists in the lump of mud, why is it (= pot) not apprehended in that state (i.e. mud-state) as it is apprehended later? Or why is its pragmatic function not present in that state, as it is present later?

[**The opponent might say:**] "That is because the particular manifestation (*vyakti*) has not arisen so far."

[**Answer**] How can you say that the pot exists (in the lump-of-mud-state)? Because that particular manifestation along with the pragmatic function etc. constitutes the pot and that form of the pot was not existent previously.

Nor is it proper to regard (two) things as one when there is a difference in their apparent forms. Because, that amounts to transgression (of reason).

† § †

२९. तस्माद् यः उपलब्धिलक्षणप्राप्तस्वभावानुपलब्धिः स नास्त्येव। न हि तस्य तत्स्वभावस्थितावनुपलब्धितः, 'अस्थितिश्चातत्त्वम्,[1] परस्परं तथास्थितयोरेव [तथास्थितयोरिव?] सुखदुःखयोरिति व्याप्तिः, असद्व्यवहारनिश्चयेन अनुपलब्धिविशेषस्य। तेनानुपलब्ध्या कस्यचिद् व्यवच्छेदं प्रसाधयता तस्य यथोक्तोपलब्धिलक्षणप्राप्तिरूपता दर्शनीया।

उपदर्शानुपलब्धिनिर्देशासमर्थनं स्वभावानुपलब्धौ, व्यापकानुपलब्धावपि धर्मयोर्व्याप्यव्यापकभावं प्रसाध्य व्यापकस्य निवृत्तिप्रसाधनं समर्थनम्।

कारणानुपलब्धावपि कार्यकारणभावं प्रसाध्य कारणस्य निवृत्ति प्रसाधनं समर्थनम्।

तद्विरुद्धोपलब्धिष्वपि द्वयोर्विरुद्धयोरेकस्य विरुद्धस्योपदर्शनं समर्थनम्।

---

१. (V); अस्थितिश्चासत्त्वम् - (R) and (D).

एवमनुपलब्धौ साधनाङ्गस्यासमर्थनं साधनाङ्गावचनम्। तद् वादिनो निग्रह-स्थानसमर्थने [? निग्रहस्थानम्, असमर्थने] तस्मिन् व्याप्यासिद्धेः।

29. **[Conclusion:]** Therefore the object, the nature of which is not apprehended but which fulfills the condition of apprehensibility is not there at all. Because, the non-apprehension is not justified when the thing exists along with that nature. Its not being (in that nature) means its not being the same thing (as itself). For example[1] pleasure and pain are mutually like that. In this way the non-apprehension of specific nature is pervaded by (= *vyāpti*) the determination of the (linguistic) practice of non-existence. Hence the one who is proving the non-existence (= *vyavaccheda*) of something on the basis of non-apprehension has to show that the object (under consideration) by its nature fulfils the condition of apprehensibility as stated above.

Having demonstrated 'the non-justification of the indication of non-apprehension (as reason)' in the case of 'non-apprehension of self-nature',[2] the justification in the case of "non-apprehension of the pervader' may be explained as proving pervaded-pervader-relation between two properties and then showing the non-existence of the pervader.

In the case of non-apprehension of cause also justification (of probans) means proving cause-effect-relation and then showing the non-existence of the cause.

In the cases of 'apprehension of the contrary' too the justification (of probans) means showing the existence of one contrary (= incompatible) object out of the two (mutually) contrary objects.

In this way non-justification of a constituent of proof in the case of non-apprehension is 'non-statement of a constituent of proof' (= *sādhanāṅgāvacana*). This is an occasion of disputant's defeat. Because, in the absence of (such a) justification, the 'pervaded' (i.e.. reason or probans) does not get proved.

† § †

३०. अथवा – साध्यते येन परेषामप्रतीतोऽर्थ इति साधनं, त्रिरूपहेतु-वचनसमुदायः। तस्याङ्गं पक्षधर्मादिवचनम्। तस्यैक-स्याप्यवचनमसाधनाङ्ग-वचनं, तदपि वादिनो निग्रहस्थानम्। तदवचने हेतुरूपस्यैवावचनम्, अवचने सिद्धेरभावात्।

30. **[Second meaning of asādhanāṅgavacana]**

Or *sādhana* (argument) means 'that by which the object not experienced by others is established', that is, 'the set of statements stating the probans with triple character.' The *aṅga* (= consutituent) of that *sādhana* is 'the statement that the probans is a characteristic (= *dharma*) of the thesis-case (= *pakṣa*)' etc. Not stating any one of them (= the three characteristics) is '*asādhanāṅgavacana*' (= non-statement of a constituent of the argument). That too is an occasion of disputant's defeat. Because not stating *sādhanāṅga* (= constituent of argument) (in this sense) is 'not stating a characteristic of probans' and if it (= a characteristic of probans) is not stated then there is no proof of the thesis.

† § †

३१. **[प्रतिज्ञादीनामसाधनाङ्गत्वम्]**

अथवा – तस्यैव साधनस्य यन्नाङ्गं प्रतिज्ञोपनयनिगमनादि तस्यासाधनाङ्गस्य साधनवाक्ये उपादानं वादिनो निग्रहस्थानं, व्यर्थाभिधानात्।

अन्वयव्यतिरेकवचनयोर्वा साधर्म्यवति वैधर्म्यवति च साधनप्रयोग एकस्यैवाभिधानेन सिद्धेर्भावाद् द्वितीयस्यासामर्थ्यमिति तस्याप्यसाधनाङ्गस्याभिधानं निग्रहस्थानं, व्यर्थाभिधानादेव।

ननु च विषयोपदर्शनाय प्रतिज्ञावचनमसाधनाङ्गमप्युपादेयमेव। न, वैयर्थ्यात्। असत्यपि प्रतिज्ञावचने यथोक्तात् साधनवाक्याद् भवत्येवेष्टार्थसिद्धिरित्यपार्थकं तस्योपादानम्।

यदि च विषयोपदर्शनमन्तरेण प्रतीतेरुत्पत्तिः, कथं न प्रतिज्ञा साधनादयः [साधनावयवः?]? न हि पक्षधर्मवचनस्यापि प्रतीतिहेतुभावादन्यः साधनार्थः, स प्रतिज्ञावचनेऽपि तुल्य इति कथं न साधनम्?

केवलस्यासामर्थ्यादसाधनत्वमिति चेत्। तत्तुल्यं पक्षधर्मवचनस्यापीति तदपि न साधनावयवः स्यात्।

न हि पक्षधर्मवचनात् केवला [केवलात्?] प्रतिपत्तेरुत्पत्तिः।

एतेन संशयोत्पत्तिः प्रत्युक्ता, पक्षधर्मवचनादपि केवलादप्रदर्शिते सम्बन्धे संशयोत्पत्तेः।

तस्माद् व्यर्थमेव साधनवाक्ये प्रतिज्ञावचनोपादानं वादिनो निग्रस्थानम्।

31. [Declaration etc. are non-constituents of proof!] [Third meaning of asādhanāṅgavacana]

Or *asādhanāṅgavacana* means employing *asādhanāṅga*, i.e., a statement which is not a proper constituent of that proof, in the statement of proof. (For instance) Declaration (= *pratijñā*), Application (of instance to the thesis-case) (= *upanaya*), conclusion (= *nigamana*) etc. (are non-constituents of proof). It is an occasion of disputant's defeat, because it is a case of unnecessary statement.

Or since the conclusion is proved by the expression of any one statement out of the statement of positive concomitance and that of negative concomitance in the argument containing similarity or dissimilarity (respectively), the statement of the other kind (of concomitance), (when one concomitance is stated), has no significant role. Hence the other statement, which is not a proper constituent of proof, is an occasion of defeat for the same reason namely unnecessary statement.

[The opponent, Naiyāyika, says:] "But it is necessary to employ the statement of Declaration in order to indicate the object (of enquiry) even if it is not a proper constituent of proof."

[Answer] No, because it is unnecessary. Because the intended object does get proved from the inferential statement as expressed above, even if the Declaration is not made. Hence employment of it (= Declaration) is without any significance.

[The opponent asks:] "Even if the (inferential) experience can be produced without indicating the object (of inference), how is not the Declaration a constituent of proof?[1] Because 'the statement that the probans characterises the thesis-case' (= *pakṣadharmavacana*) does not have any other purpose in proof apart from causing the (inferential) experience. And the same purpose lies behind the Declaration also. How is (= Declaration) not the (part of) proof then?"

[The Buddhist might answer:] "Declaration alone is not capable (of proving the probandum) and hence does not constitute the proof."

[The opponent responds:] "The case is common with the statement of probans characterising thesis case. So that statement too would be a non-constituent of proof. Because the (inferential) cognition cannot be produced merely from the statement of probans characterising thesis-case."

[The author's answer:] (The statement of probans characterising thesis-case along with the statement of pervasion constitutes the proof. But that is not the case with the Declaration. Declaration along with the statement of pervasion does not constitute the proof.)[2] This answers the arisal of doubt (in the case of Declaration), because the doubt (about the

> probandum) can arise from the mere statement of probans characterising the thesis case, when the relation (of pervasion) is not shown.

Therefore the employment of the statement of Declaration is definitely unnecessary and is the occasion of disputant's defeat.

† § †

३२. अथवा साधनस्य सिद्धेर्यन्नाङ्गम् - असिद्धः, विरुद्धः अनैकान्तिको वा हेत्वाभासः तस्यापि वचनं वादिनो निग्रहस्थानम्, असमर्थोपादानात्।

तथा साध्यादिविकलस्य अन्वयाप्रदर्शितान्वया तैरपि [? अनन्वया-प्रदर्शितान्वयादेरपि] दृष्टान्ताभासस्य साधनाङ्गस्य [? असाधनाङ्गस्य] वचनमपि वादिनो निग्रहस्थानम् असमर्थोपादानादेव। न हि तैर्हेतोः सम्बन्धः शक्यते प्रदर्शयितुम्। अप्रदर्शनादसामर्थ्यम्।

32. **[Fourth meaning of asādhanāṅgavacana]**

Or *asādhanāṅgavacana* means the statement of what is not the constituent of *sādhana*, i.e., proof. For instance the fallacious probans such as Unproved, Contrary or Inconclusive probans (is like that). This too is the occasion of disputant's defeat, because it amounts to the employment of something incapable (of proving the probandum).

Likewise, a statement of a fallacious instance, which is not a constituent of proof, is also an occasion of disputant's defeat. For example, '(Positive) instance lacking probandum-property' etc.; '(Positive) instance without positive concomitance', '(Positive) instance without the indication of the positive concomitance' etc. They are occasions of defeat for the same reason, viz., that they amount to employment of something incapable (of proving the probandum). Because such fallacious instances cannot demonstrate the relation of probans (with the probandum); and because they do not demonstrate (the relation), they are incapable (of playing their role in the proof).

† § †

३३. अथवा - सिद्धिः साधनं, तदङ्गं धर्मो यस्यार्थस्य विवादाश्रयस्य वादप्रस्तावहेतोः स साधनाङ्गः। तद्व्यतिरेकेणापरस्याप्यजिज्ञासितस्य विशेषस्या-शास्त्राश्रयव्याजादिभिः प्रक्षेपो मोषणं [घोषणं?] च परव्यामोहनानुभाषण-शक्तिविघातादिहेतोः, तदप्यसाधनाङ्गवचनं वादिनो निग्रहस्थानम्, अप्रस्तुताभिधानात्।

एभिः कथाविच्छेद एव; तथा विशेषसहितस्यार्थस्य प्रतिवादिनोऽ-जिज्ञासितत्वात्। जिज्ञासायामदोषः। जिज्ञासितं पुनरर्थस्यान्यस्य प्रसङ्गपरंपरया ये ष पन्नादिना (?) बहिः प्रतिवादिनः, प्राश्निकानां च न्यायदर्शिनामिति।

एभिः कथाविच्छेद एव करणीयः। न हि कश्चिदर्थः क्वचित् क्रियमाणप्रसङ्गे न प्रयुज्यते, नैरात्म्यवादिनस्तु तत्साधने नृत्यगीत्यादेरपि तत्र प्रसङ्गात्।

यथा - प्रतिज्ञाभिधानपूर्वकं कश्चित् कुर्यात् - 'नास्त्यात्मा' इति वयं बौद्धा ब्रूमः। के बौद्धाः? ये बुद्धस्य भगवतः शासनमभ्युपगताः। को बुद्धो भगवान्? यस्य शासने भदन्ताश्वघोषः प्रव्रजितः। क : पुनर्भदन्ताश्वघोषः? यस्य राष्ट्रपालं नाम नाटकम्। कीदृशं राष्ट्रपालं नाम नाटकम्? इति प्रसङ्गं कृत्वा 'नान्द्यन्ते ततः प्रविशति सूत्रधारः' इति पठेत्, नृत्येद्, गायेच्च। प्रतिवादी तं च सर्वप्रसङ्गं नानुकर्तुं समर्थ इति पराजितः स्यात्। इति सभ्यः साधुसम्मतानां विदुषां तत्त्वचिन्ताप्रकारः!

33. **(Fifth meaning of asādhanāṅgavacana)**

Or *sādhana* means proof. And *sādhanāṅga* means the object which has the proof as its *aṅga* meaning characteristic. That is, the object which is the basis (or root) of the debate, (that is,) which causes the proposal of debate is called *sādhanāṅga*. So *asādhanāṅga* also means expressing and announcing some special subject different from *sādhanāṅga,* not enquired by the opponent, under the pretext of claiming that he (= the opponent) is not following the discipline (= *śāstra*). This is done with the intention of confusing the opponent and impeding his power to repeat (the statement made by the disputant) etc. This too is *asādhanāṅgavacana* and is the occasion of disputant's defeat, because it amounts to irrelevant statement.

Such occurrences do amount to breaking the discussion. Because the object as qualified by that special characteristic was not enquired by the opponent. If there is an enquiry (about it) then there is no fault. That the characteristic is enquired means that it is enquired by the opponent and by enquirers (= arbitrators) who know logic,[1] by drawing a series of implications.

On the occurrence of them (= such irrelevant statements) the discussion should be broken. Because (otherwise) nothing is inapplicable in some made-up context. The upholder of No-self-doctrine, for instance, while proving his doctrine could even dance and sing (and that will have to be regarded as relevant)!

It could happen as follows: One will make a Declaration and perform as follows - "There is no self." We the Buddhists say this. Who are the Buddhists? Those are the Buddhists who take recourse to the teaching of the Lord Buddha. Who is the Lord Buddha? Lord Buddha is the one, on following whose teaching the Buddhist Aśvaghoṣa became a monk. Who is the Buddhist Aśvaghoṣa? The author of the play called '*Rāṣṭrapāla*'. What sort of a play is '*Rāṣṭrapāla*'? By creating an occasion (in this way) the disputant should read "After the Prologue enters the Director" and then should dance and sing. The opponent being incapable of imitating the whole performance will be defeated. What a courteous way of philosphising followed by the well-recognised savants![2]

३४. न चैवं प्रस्तुतस्य पर्यवसानं स भवति [? सम्भवति], 'अनिश्चय'[१]-फलत्वादनारम्भ एव वादस्य।

कथं चैव जयपराजयौ? प्रतिवादिनोऽप्यननुभाषणस्यैवम्प्रकारस्य प्रसङ्गस्य विस्तरेणानुभाषणव्याजेन सम्भवाद्, अनिश्चितत्वाच्च।

तस्मात् प्रतिज्ञावचनमेव तावन्न न्याय्यम्। कुतः पुनस्तत्राजिज्ञासितविशेष-प्रसङ्गोपन्यासः, तद्व्याख्याप्रसङ्गवितथप्रलापश्च?

सर्वश्चायं प्रकारो दुर्मतिभिः शठैर्न्यायसामर्थ्येनार्थप्रतिपादनेऽसमर्थैः प्रवर्तितः।

यथा – 'पुरुषातिशयपूर्वकाणि तनुभुवनकरणादीनि' इति प्रतिज्ञाय तनुकरणभुवनव्याख्याव्याजेन सकलवैशेषिकशास्त्रार्थघोषणम्।

'नित्यः शब्दोऽनित्यो वा' इति वादे द्वादशलक्षणप्रपञ्चप्रकाशनशास्त्र 'प्रणेतृ'[२]-जैमिनिप्रतिज्ञाततत्त्वनित्यताधिकरणशब्दघटान्यतरसद्वितीयो घटः इति प्रतिज्ञामुपरचय्य द्वादशलक्षणादिव्याख्यानम्।

सर्वोऽयं दुर्मतीनामसामर्थ्यप्रच्छादनोपायः, न तु सत्यैरस्त्युपेतः, तत्त्वपरीक्षायां फलादिप्रतिसरणदण्डप्रयोगादीनामयुक्तत्वात्।

34. The proposed topic cannot get concluded in this way because determination (of truth) is the (proper) result of a debate. But (here) there is no beginning of the debate at all. How are victory and defeat possible in this way? Because the opponent himself too can give another performance under the pretext of repeating the disputant's performance and create a situation of 'Non-reproduction' of this kind.[1] Secondly there will be no determination (of truth) in this situation.

Therefore stating the Declaration itself is not reasonable. What to say of opening some special topics which are not

---

१. (R); निश्चय – (D).

२. (V); प्रणेतुः – (D).

enquired? And what to say of the futile chattering under the pretext of explaining that topic?

This whole (unreasonable) way has been introduced by malignant and deceitful persons incapable of stating things with the strength of logic.

For example one first makes the Declaration: "Body, earth, instruments etc. are preceded by excellence of a Self" and then announces the whole of Vaiśeṣika discipline under the pretext of explaining the terms 'body', 'instruments' and 'earth'.

Or in the debate over the question whether sound is permanent or impermanent, one makes a Declaration: "Pot is coupled with either of the two things viz. sound and pot, out of which sound is the locus of 'permanence', which is a category declared by Jaimini, who was the author of the discipline, which illuminates the explanation of twelve definitions." And then one goes on explaining the twelve definitions etc.

All this is a device used by malignant people for hiding their incapability. It is not accompanied by truths. Because (for instance), the practices such as offering fruits etc. and application of rods etc. are improper in a critical examination of Truth.[2]

† § †

३५. भवत्येव नाटकादिघोषणेऽर्थान्तरगमनात् पराजय इति चेत्, अन्यस्याप्य-जिज्ञासितस्य किं न भवति? न हि तस्यापि काचिद् विवक्षितसाध्यधर्मसिद्धौ नान्तरीयकता। यथा हेतुप्रत्ययपारतन्त्र्यलक्षणसंस्कारदुःखतादिसिद्धिमन्तरेण नानित्यतासिद्धिः।

तथाविधस्तु धर्मः पृथगनुक्तोऽपि साध्यधर्मेऽन्तर्भावात् पक्षीकृत एवेति न पृथगस्योपन्यासः, व्याख्यानं वा। तस्मादेवंविधस्यापि तदानीं 'प्रतिवादिनो जिज्ञासितस्यार्थस्य' प्रतिज्ञायामन्यत्रैवोपन्यासो व्याख्यानं वा अर्थान्तरगमन।न्निग्रहस्थानमेव।

तेन जिज्ञासितधर्ममात्रमेव साधनाङ्गं वाच्यं, न प्रसङ्ग उपक्षेप्तव्यः, तदुपक्षेपेऽतिप्रसङ्गात्।

एवमसाधनाङ्गवचनं वादिनो निग्रहस्थानं प्रतिवादिना तथाभावे प्रतिपादिते, अन्यथा द्वयोरेकस्यापि न जयपराजयाविति।

35. **[The opponent might say:]** "One gets defeated by announcing a drama (and performing it) etc. in a debate (, but that is so) because there one shifts to a different topic."

[**Answer**] Does not the same thing happen if one announces some other thing which is not enquired? That other thing too has no invariable relation with the proof of the intended probandum-property, as (for instance, there *is* an invariable relation in the following case:) impermanence (of composite objects) does not get proved unless the unpleasantness of composite objects, that is, their dependence upon cause and other conditions is proved.[1]

But although such a characteristic (of probandum) (which is relevant to the proof of the probandum) is not stated separately, it is not to be presented or explained separately either. Because, as it is included in the probandum-property, is becomes (a part of the) thesis itself.

१. प्रतिवादिनोऽजिज्ञासितस्यार्थस्य is probably more consistent with the context.

Therefore (separate) presentation or explanation even of such a (relevant) characteristic which is not enquired by the opponent,[2] made during Declaration or some other time is definitely an occasion of defeat because it is a case of shifting to a Different Topic.

Therefore only that constituent of the proof should be uttered which refers to the inquired characteristic (of probandum). No allied topic (= *prasaṅga*) should be opened. Because, if we open it, then there would be transgression (of the rules of debate).

Hence *asādhanāṅgavacana* (in any of the senses stated above) is the occasion of disputant's defeat, when it is shown to be so by the opponent. Otherwise (i.e. if it is not shown to be so by the opponent) then there will be neither victory nor defeat of any of the two debaters.[3]

† § †

३६. [अदोषोद्भावनं निग्रहस्थानम्]

अदोषोद्भावनं प्रतिवादिनो निग्रहस्थानम्। वादिना साधने प्रत्युक्तेऽभ्युपगतोत्तरपक्षो यत्र विषये प्रतिवादी यदा न दोषमुद्भावयति, तदा पराजितो वक्तव्यः।

साधनदोषाः पुनः - न्यूनत्वम्, असिद्धिः, अनैकान्तिकता, वादिनः साधयितुमिष्टस्यार्थस्य विपर्ययसाधनम्, अष्टादश दृष्टान्ताभासाश्च। तेषामनुद्भावनमप्रतिपादनं प्रतिवादिनः पराजयाधिकरणम्।

'तत्'[1] पुनः साधनस्य निर्दोषत्वात्, सदोषत्वेऽपि प्रतिवादिनोऽज्ञानात्, प्रतिपादनासामर्थ्याद् वा।

न हि दुष्टसाधनाभिधानेऽपि वादिनः प्रतिवादिनोऽप्रतिपादिते दोषे पराजयव्यवस्थापना युक्ता, तयोरेव परस्परसामर्थ्योपघातापेक्षया जयपराजय-व्यवस्थापनात्।

केवलं हेत्वाभासाद् भूतप्रतिपत्तेरभावाद प्रतिपादकस्य जयोऽपि नास्त्येव। न हि तत्त्वचिन्तायां कश्चिच्छलव्यवहारः।

यद्येवं, किंनु पराजयः, तत्त्वसिद्धिभ्रंशात्? न, अनिराकरणात्। निराकरणं हि तस्यान्येन पराजयः, न सिद्ध्यभावः, 'प्रतियोग्यपेक्षणात्। सिद्ध्यभावस्य'[2] साधनाभावेऽसत्यपि प्रतियोगिनि भावात्। प्रतियोगिनश्च तन्निराकरणेऽ सामर्थ्यात् पराजयस्यानुत्पत्तेरपराजयः।

तस्मादयमसमर्थसाधनाभिधाय्यपि परेण तथाभावेऽप्रतिपादितेऽपराजितो वक्तव्यः।

36. [Adoṣodbhāvana as an occasion of defeat]

Adoṣodbhāvana, i.e., not pointing out the fault (of the disputant) is the occasion of opponent's defeat. When the disputant presents the proof, but the opponent who has accepted the opposite view, does not point out any fault in (the argument pertaining to) the object of enquiry,[1] then the opponent is to be called defeated.

The faults in proof are (1) Deficiency (2) Unprovedness (3) Inconclusiveness (4) the probans proving contrary of the object intended by the disputant to prove and (5-22) the eighteen fallacies of instance. Not pointing them out, i.e. not indicating them is the ground of opponent's defeat.

---

१. (R); ततः - (D).

२. This is more consistent. But प्रतियोग्यपेक्षणात् सिद्ध्यभावस्य। - (D).

This[2] (occasion of defeat) takes place either because the proof (given by the disputant) is without any fault or because the proof is faulty but the opponent does not understand the fault or because he (= opponent) is incapable of indicating it.

Even if the disputant states a fallacious proof, it is not proper to ascertain the defeat (of the disputant) in case the fault (in the proof) is not indicated by the opponent. Because the ascertainment of victory and defeat is relative to vitiating each other's capasity.

Nor does the one (= the opponent) who does notindicate (the fault of the disputant) get victory only on account of fallacious probans (stated by the disputant) because the knowledge of truth is not (reached by any one) there. Because, no practice of cheating is in order in a philosophical enquiry.

[**The opponent might ask:**] "If that is the case (i.e. if the opponent cannot be declared as having won if he does not discover the disputant's fault), would it be the case of (disputant's) defeat then? Because, he (= the disputant) has failed to establish the truth."

[**Answer**] No, because here the repudiation (of disputant's argument) does not take place. Because, his (= disputant's) defeat by the other debater consists in the repudiation (of his argument by the other defeater). It does not consist in his not establishing (the truth). Because, it (= defeat) requires the (presence of an) opponent. Because, there can be absence of (a sound) proof when there is no (sound) probans, even if there is no opponent. So there is no defeat, because there is no occurrence thereof, because the opponent is incapable of repudicating (the disputant's argument). Therefore even if the disputant states an inadequate (= *asamartha*) proof, he is to be called non-defeated if the inadequateness of the proof is not indicated by the opponent.

† § †

३७. **[वादे छलव्यवहारनिषेधः]**

छलव्यवहारोऽपि विजिगीषूणां वाद इति चेत्। न, दुर्जनविप्रतिपत्त्यधिकारे सतां शास्त्रप्रवृत्तेः। न हि परानुग्रहप्रवृत्ता मिथ्याप्रलापारम्भात् सोत्कर्षपरपंसनादीन् [स्वोत्कर्षपरपंसनादीन् ?] असद्व्यवहारान् उपदिशन्ति। न च परविपंसनेन लाभसत्कारश्लोकोपार्जनं सतामाचारः।

नापि तथाप्रवृत्तेभ्यः स्वहस्तदानेन प्राणिनामुपतापनं सत्सम्मतानां शास्त्रकार सभासदां युक्तम्। न च न्यायशास्त्राणि सद्भिर्लाभाद्युपार्जनाय प्रणीयन्ते।

तस्मान्न योगविहितः कश्चिद् विजिगीषुवादो नाम। परानुग्रहप्रवृत्तास्तु सन्तो विप्रतिपन्नं प्रतिपादयन्तो न्यायमनुसरेयुः सत्साधनाभिधानेन, भूतदोषोद्भावनेन वा।

साक्षिप्रत्यक्षं तस्यैवानुप्रबोधाय। तदेव न्यायानुसरणं सतां वादः - उक्तन्याये तत्त्वार्थी चेत् 'प्रतिपद्येत,'[१] तदप्रतिपत्तावप्यन्यो न विप्रतिपद्येतेति।

तत्त्वरक्षणार्थं सद्भिरुपहर्तव्यमेव छलादि विजिगीषुभिरिति चेत्। नखचपेटशस्त्रप्रहारादीपनादिभिरपीति वक्तव्यम्! तस्मान्न ज्यायानयं तत्त्वरक्षणोपायः।

साधनप्रख्यापनं सतां तत्त्वरक्षणोपायः, साधनाभासदूषणं च। तदभावे मिथ्याप्रलापादत्र परोपतापविधानेऽपि तत्त्वाप्रतिष्ठापनात्। अन्यथापि न्यायोपवर्णने विद्वत्प्रतिष्ठानात्।

---

१. (R); प्रतिपद्येतेति - (D).

तस्मात् परानुग्रहाय तत्त्वख्यापनं वादिनो विजयः, भूतदोषदर्शनेन मिथ्याप्रतिपत्तिनिवर्तनं प्रतिवादिनः।

37. **[Prohibition of cheating - practices in debate]**

[A possible objection:] "But the practice of cheating can be (an acceptable part of) debate between persons desirious of victory!"

[Answer] No, Because, any science written by noble persons operates in its proper domain (= *adhikāra*), namely, the misconceptions of ignoble persons. (It operates in order to remove these misconceptions.) Persons inclined to favour others do not (themselves) prescribe ignoble practices like elevating oneself and spoiling others[1] by starting false chattering. Gaining profit, felicitation and fame by spoiling others is not a conduct of noble persons. Nor is it proper for the members of the assembly, who are experts in the science (of debate) (Lit. authors of the science; śāstrakāra) and who are recognised by noble persons, to trouble creatures by giving a helping hand to those who are inclined in that way (i.e. inclined to use cheating techniques in debate). Moreover, the scientific works on logic are not created by noble persons in order to gain profit etc.

Therefore, there is no such thing as a legitimate debate between persons desirous of victory.[2] The noble persons, on the other hand, who are inclined to favour others, should follow logic while stating (their arguments) to the persons having misconception (about truth), either by stating a sound probans or by pointing out the real fault (of the opponent). Witnesses' observation is also meant for enlightening the same (kind of practice). The same act of following logic is the debate of noble persons. (It follows the dictum:) When the reasoning is stated (by one debater), he (= the other debater) should understand it, if he wants to know the truth; and even if he does not understand it, (at least) someone else (say, the audience) should not apprehend it wrongly.[3]

[A Naiyāyika might object:] "The noble persons desirous of victory should certainly employ quibbling and other techniques for protecting the truth."

[Answer] In that case you should also say that (one should try to protect the truth) also by means of hitting with nails, slaps and weapons or by blazing him up! Therefore this means to protection of truth is no better.

The noble person's means to protection of truth is: presenting the (sound) proof and refuting the fallacious proof. Because, the truth does not get established in the absence of them, even if the other person is perturbed by making false chattering. If (on the other hand) one describes (the truth) logically, then he is respected amongst learned persons even without it (i.e. even without perturbing the other debater by way of false chattering).

Therefore establishing truth for favouring others is the victory of the disputant and preventing false conception by showing real faults is the victory of the opponent.

† § †

३८. अथवा – यो न दोषः साधनस्य, तद्भावेऽपि वादिना तदसाधयितुम् [तदा साधयितुम् ?] इष्टस्यार्थस्य सिद्धेर्विघाताभावात्, तस्योद्भावनं प्रतिवादिनो निग्रहाधिकरणं, मिथ्योत्तराभिधानात्। यथा साध्यतयाऽनिष्टोऽपि वादिनो धर्मः शास्त्रोपगमात् साध्य इति तद्विपर्यासेन न विरोधोद्भावनम्।

'नास्त्यात्मा' इति तव प्रतिज्ञापदयोर्विरोध इति प्रतिज्ञादोषोद्भावनं, 'प्रयत्नान्तरीयकः शब्दोऽनित्यः, प्रयत्नान्तरीयकत्वाद्' इति हेतोर्धर्मविशेषत्वात् प्रतिज्ञार्थैकदेश इत्यसिद्धोद्भावनं, सर्वाणि साधर्म्यवैधर्म्यसमादीनि जात्युत्तराणि इत्येवमादेर्दोषस्योद्भावनमदोषोद्भावनम्। तस्य वादिना दोषाभासत्वे प्रख्यापिते प्रतिवादी पराजितो वक्तव्यः, पूर्वपक्षे साधनस्य निर्दोषत्वात्।

दोषवति पुनः साधने न द्वयोरेकस्यापि जयपराजयौ, तत्त्वाप्रख्यापनात्, अदोषोद्भावनं च। अप्रतिपक्षायां च पक्षसिद्धौ कृतायां जेता भवति।

तस्माज्जिगीषता स्वपक्षश्च स्थापनीयः, परपक्षश्च निराकर्तव्यः।

निर्दोषे साधनाभिधानेऽपि वादिनः प्रतिवादिना दोषाभास उद्भाविते दूषणाभावत्वख्यापने एव जयपराजयौ, नान्यथा, भावतस्तत्त्वाभिधानेऽपि प्रतिपक्षनिराकरणेन तत्त्वस्य प्रख्यापनासामर्थ्यात्, न प्रतिवादिनोऽप्यत्र, भावतो मिथ्याप्रतिपत्तेरिति।

इदं न्याय्यं निग्रहस्थानलक्षणमुक्तमस्माभिः।

38. **[Second meaning of adoṣodbhāvana]**

Or (*adoṣodbhāvana* means) pointing out that (as a fault) which is not the (real) fault in the proof. Because, in spite of the presence of that (= the accused fault), there is no harm in the establishment of the object intended to be proved by the disputant. It is a ground of opponent's defeat because it is a case of giving a false answer. For example, some property which is not intended to be proved by the disputant is claimed (by the opponent) to be provable, on the ground that it is accepted in the disputant's system

(= *śāstra*), and then its contrariety (with the probans) is shown At that time the fallacy of contrariety is not (really) brought out (by the opponent).

(Other examples of *adoṣodbhāvāna* are)- (1) Pointing out the fault of Declaration in (the Declaration:) "Self does not exist" by saying that the terms in your Declaration are mutually contradictory. (2) Pointing out the fallacy of unproved probans in the argument, "The sound generated through efforts is impermanent because it is generated through efforts" saying that this probans is a specific characteristic (of the probandum) and hence a part of the Declaration. (3) All the analogical responses (= *jātyuttara*; psendo-refutations)[1] referred to (in *Nyāyasūtra*) as: "*Sādharmyasama, Vaidharmyasama* etc. are the analogical responses." Pointing out (pseudo) faults of this kind is *adoṣodbhāvana* (= pointing out non-fault as fault). When it is shown to be a pseudo-fault by the disputant, the opponent should be declared as defeated, because the probans (employed) in the first position (by the disputant) is faultless.

But if the probans (or argument) (used by the disputant) is faulty, neither of the two parties has gained either victory or defeat. Because that (faulty) character (of the probans or the argument) has not been shown and yet a non-fault has been pointed out (as fault).[2] One becomes a winner when one establishes one's position and there is no contrary position.

Therefore the person desirous of victory should establish his own position and repudiate the position of the other.

Even when the disputant states a faultless proof and the opponent points out a pseudo-fault, victory and defeat can be declared only when it is shown that there is no (real) fault, not otherwise. Because, in the latter case although the disputant in fact states the truth, he is unable to show the truth by repudiating the contrary position. Nor does the opponent win here because he (= the opponent) has in fact a false understanding.

So we have stated this logically proper definition of 'occasion of defeat.'

† § †

Part II

न्यायमतखण्डनम्

Refutation of the *Nyāya*-View

३९. अन्यत्तु न युक्तमिति नेष्यते। यत्रेदं यथोक्तं निग्रहस्थानलक्षणं नास्ति, तस्य निग्रहस्थानत्वमयुक्तमिति नोक्तमस्माभिः।

[१.] "प्रतिदृष्टान्तधर्माभ्यनुज्ञा स्वदृष्टान्ते प्रतिज्ञाहानिः निग्रहस्थानम्" [न्या. सू. ५.२.२] इत्यत्र भाष्यकारमतं दूषयित्वा वार्तिककारो यं स्थितपक्षमाह, तत्रैवं ब्रूमः – प्रतिदृष्टान्तस्य यो धर्मस्तं यदा स्वदृष्टान्तेऽभ्यनुजानाति निगृहीतो वेदितव्यः।

तत्र दृष्टश्चासावन्ते च व्यवस्थित इति दृष्टान्तः। स्वदृष्टान्तःस्वपक्षः। प्रतिदृष्टान्तः प्रतिपक्षः। प्रतिपक्षस्य धर्मं स्वपक्षेऽभ्यनुजानन् पराजितः। यथा 'अनित्यः शब्द ऐन्द्रियकत्वाद्' इति ब्रुवन् प्रतिपक्षवादिनि सामान्येन प्रत्यवस्थिते आह – 'यदि सामान्यमैन्द्रियकं नित्यं शब्दोऽप्येवमस्तु' इत्येषा प्रतिज्ञाहानिः, प्राक्प्रतिज्ञातस्य शब्दानित्यत्वस्य त्यागादिति।

39. (The second half of the first verse is:) "Any other occasion of defeat, however, is not just; hence we do not accept it". This means: The character of being an occasion

of defeat does not apply properly where the definition of 'occasion of defeat' as stated by us is not applicable. So we have not attributed that character to them.

(1) **[Pratijñāhāni:** Declaration-abandonment]

"'Declaration-abandonment' means admitting a property of the counter-position (= *pratidṛṣṭānta*) in one's own position (= *dṛṣṭānta*)". [*N.S.*. 5.2.2.] The author of *Nyāya-vārtika* (i.e. Udyotakava) while writing on this aphorism repudiates the opinion of the author of *Nyāya-bhāṣya* (i.e. Vātsyāyana) and states his finished position. We say on this as follows-

[Udyotakara has said[1]:] "Where the disputant admits the property of *prati-dṛṣṭānta* in one's own *dṛṣṭānta* he is to be known as defeated. In this *'dṛṣṭānta'* means that which is seen and established at the end (of the argument). One's own *dṛṣṭānta* means one's own position. And *'pratidṛṣṭānta'* means the counter-position. So the one who admits a characteristic of counter-position in one's own position is defeated. For example when the debater who says "Sound is impermanent because it is knowable through senses" is countered by the opponent by pointing out 'universal' (= *sāmānya*) (as the counter-instance), he (= the former debater) says, "If universal is knowable through senses and is permanent, let the sound also be like that. This is a case of Declaration - abandonment because here one abandons the impermanence of sound which one has declared before."

†§†

४०. अत्रोपगतप्रतिज्ञात्यागात् प्रतिज्ञाहानौ विशेषप्रतिनियमः किंकृतोऽनेन प्रकारेण प्रतिज्ञां त्यजतः प्रतिज्ञाहानिरिति।

सम्भवति ह्यनेनापि प्रकारेण हेतुदोषोद्भावनादिना प्रतिपक्षसाधनाभिधानेन च स्वपक्षपरित्यागः, परपक्षोपगमश्च।

इदमेव च प्रतिज्ञाहानेः प्रधानं निमित्तम्। एवं प्रतिपादितेन प्रतिज्ञा हातव्या, हानौ च पराजय इति।

40. **[Dharmakīrti's response:]**

If Declaration-abandonment occurs here because the Declaration once accepted is abandoned, then why is this special restriction made that Declaration-abandonment is attributed to one who abandons Declaration *in this way* (i.e. in the way stated by you)?

Because, it could occur in this way also: when the fault in one's probans etc. is pointed out and the proof of the counter-position is stated (by the opponent), there is abandonment of one's own position and admission of the opponent's position.

In fact this is the main cause of abandoning one's own Declaration. When one is answered (by the opponent) in the above way, one has to abandon one's Declaration and when one abandons it, one is defeated.

† § †

४१. इदं पुनरसम्बद्धमेव – 'सामान्यं नित्यमैन्द्रियकम्' इत्युक्ते 'शब्दोऽप्येवमस्तु' इति कः स्वस्थात्मा स्वयमैन्द्रियकत्वादनित्यः शब्दो घटवदिति ब्रुवन् सामान्येनोपदर्शनमात्रेण नित्यं शब्दं प्रतिपद्येत?

सामान्यस्यापि नित्यस्यैन्द्रियकत्वे तस्यानित्ये घटे दर्शनात् संशयितः स्यात्। जात्या प्रतिपद्येतापीति चेत्। तथापि किं सामान्योपदर्शनेन?

एवमेव नित्यः शब्दः इति वक्तव्यम्, जडस्य प्रतिपत्तौ विचाराभावात्।

न च नित्यसामान्योपदर्शनेन तद्धर्मं शब्दे प्रतिपद्यमानेन प्रतिपक्षधर्मोऽभ्यनुज्ञातो भवति। 'अनित्यः शब्दः' इति च वदतो नित्यशब्द 'इत्याञ्जसः'[१] प्रतिपक्षः स्यात्,

१. (V); इत्याभासः - (R) and (D).

न नित्यं सामान्यमिति।

तस्मादैन्द्रियकत्वस्य नित्यानित्यपक्षवृत्तेर्व्यभिचारादसाधनाङ्गस्योपादाना-न्निग्रहार्हः, न प्रतिपक्षधर्मानुज्ञयाऽनेन प्रकारेण प्रतिज्ञाहानेः।

41. "When one (= the opponent) says that the universal is knowable through senses and is permanent, (the disputant would say,) "Let the sound also be like that." This statement of yours is quite inappropriate here. Because, which sound-hearted person, who himself argues that sound is impermanent because it is knowable through senses like a pot, would admit that sound is permanent merely on the basis of an (opposite) instance viz. 'universal'?

If universal, which is permanent, is knowable through senses, the probans viz. 'knowability through senses' will be doubtful (i.e. Inconclusive), because it is seen in the impermanent pot (also).

[A possible objection:] "The disputant could admit (that the sound is permanent) on the basis of analogical argument (= *jāti*)"[1]

[Answer] What is the need of presenting 'universal' as the instance then?

One (i.e. the opponent) should better say "sound is permanent" (This would suffice to make the disputant admit the counter-thesis) Because an insensitive person does not think while admitting (anything).

Moreover, the characteristic of counter-thesis does not happen to be accepted by the one who admits a characteristic of the (counter - instance viz.) universal as a characteristic of sound when the permanent universal is presented as an (opposite) instance.

The closest (= *āñjasaḥ*) counter-thesis for the disputant who says, 'Sound is impermanent' is 'Sound is permanent' and not 'Universal is permanent'.

Therefore (in this case) the disputant is worthy of defeat because he employes a non-consituent of proof, because 'knowability through senses', which exists in permanent as well as impermanent things, has variable relation (with the probandum viz. impermanence). He is *not* worthy of defeat because of abandoning the Declaration in this way by accepting some characteristic of the counter-thesis.

† § †

४२. [2.] "प्रतिज्ञातार्थप्रतिषेधे धर्मविकल्पात् तदर्थनिर्देश: प्रतिज्ञान्तरम्।" [न्या. सू. 5.2.3] प्रतिज्ञातोऽर्थोऽनित्य: शब्द ऐन्द्रियकत्वादित्येव, तस्य हेतुव्यभिचारोपदर्शनेन प्रतिषेधे कृते धर्मभेदविकल्पात् सामान्यघटयो: सर्वगतत्वासर्वगतत्वधर्मविकल्पेन प्रतिज्ञान्तरं करोति - यथा घटोऽसर्वगतोऽनित्य:, एवं शब्दोऽप्यसर्वगतोऽनित्य इति। एतत्प्रतिज्ञान्तरं नाम निग्रहस्थानं साधनसामर्थ्येऽप्यपरिज्ञानात्। स हि पूर्वस्या: 'अनित्य: शब्द:' इति प्रतिज्ञाया: साधनात्तदा याम् 'असर्वगत: शब्द' इति प्रतिज्ञामाह, तद्दर्शनाय तदर्थनिर्देश इत्याह। तदर्थ: 'पूर्वोक्तसाध्यसिद्ध्यर्थ:'[१]। उत्तरप्रतिज्ञानिर्देशस्तदर्थनिर्देश:। न च प्रतिज्ञा प्रतिज्ञान्तरसाधने समर्था, इति निग्रहस्थानम्।

42. (2) [**Pratijñāntara**: Another Declaration]

"'Another Declaration' means indicating that the object of Declaration possesses another (probandum)-characteristic; when the declared object is repudiated (by the opponent)." (*N.S.* 5.2.3)

---

१. (R); पूर्वोक्तसाध्यसिद्ध्यर्थम् - (D).

[**Naiyāyikas explain:**] "The declared object is "Sound is impermanent because knowable through senses." When it is repudiated by presenting the variable relation of probans (with the probandum), one (= the disputant) makes another Declaration by attributing another characteristic, when he imagines the characteristics viz. ubiquitousness and non-ubiquitousness in the cases of universal and pot (respectively) in the following way - 'Just as pot is non-ubiquitous and impermanent, sound too is non-ubiquitous and impermanent.' This is the occasion of defeat called 'Another Declaration', because although the probans was sound, the disputant did not comprehend it (= its soundness)."

"Here he (= the author of the aphorism) uses the expression 'indicating the object of that' (= *tadarthanirdeśaḥ*) for referring to the Declaration, 'Sound is non-ubiquitious' which the disputant states after giving a proof for the first Declaration, 'Sound is impermanent'. Here (in the expression 'indicating the object of that') 'the object of that' (= *tadarthaḥ*) means the object of the proof of the probandum stated before. Indicating the object of that means indicating the later Declaration. And it is an occasion of defeat because one Declaration is not capable of proving another Declaration."[1]

† § †

४३. अत्रापि नैवं ब्रुवता प्रतिज्ञान्तरं पूर्वप्रतिज्ञासाधनायोक्तं भवति। किं तर्हि? विशेषणम्। ऐन्द्रियकत्वस्य हेतोः सामान्ये वृत्त्या व्यभिचार उद्भावितेऽसर्वगतत्वे सत्यैन्द्रियकत्वस्य हेतोर्विशेषणोपादाने व्यभिचारं परिहरति, न पुनः प्रतिज्ञान्तरमाह; असर्वगतत्वस्य शब्दे सिद्धत्वात्. प्रतिज्ञायाश्च साध्यनिर्देशलक्षणत्वात्।

यदप्युक्तं – 'पूर्वं प्रतिज्ञासाधनायोत्तरां प्रतिज्ञामाह' इति, तदप्ययुक्तम्। न हि प्रतिज्ञा प्रतिज्ञासाधनायोच्यमाना प्रतिज्ञान्तरं भवति। किं तर्हि? हेत्वादेरन्यतमः साध्यसाधनायोपादानात्। साधननिर्देशः स स्यात्, न साध्यनिर्देशः।

उदाहरणसाधर्म्यादेश्च हेतुलक्षणस्यासर्वगतत्वे भावात्, प्रतिज्ञालक्षणस्य चाभावात्। हेतुत्वमसर्वगतत्वे प्रयुक्तं न प्रतिज्ञान्तरम्।

43. **[Dharmakīrti's criticism:]** In this statement too the one (= the disputant) who replies as stated above does not make another Declaration for proving earlier Declaration but he states only a qualification (of probans). When the variable relation of the probans viz. 'knowability through senses' (with the probandum viz. impermanence) is pointed out by indicating the existence of the probans in the universals, the disputant removes the 'variability of the relation' by employing a qualification of probans as 'knowability-through-senses qualified by non-ubiquitousness'. But he does not make another Declaration, because non-ubiquitousness is proved in the case of sound and 'Declaration' is defined as 'indication of the provable' (= *sādhya*) (and not as indication of the proved).

What has been said (by you), namely, 'One makes the later Declaration for proving earlier Declaration' is also wrong. Because the Declaration which is stated for proving another Declaration does not become (the occasion of defeat called). 'Another Declaration'. But it is one of the elements such as probans etc. (stated additionally for proving the first Declaration), (which becomes on occasion of defeat) because it is this element which is employed here for proving the probandum. But it (= employment of a different probans etc.) will be the indication of the probans, and not the indication of the provable.

This is so also because the defining characteristic of a probans such as 'similarity with the instance'[1] is present in 'non-ubiquitousness' but the defining characteristic of

Declaration is not present in it. And the probans-hood attributed to 'non-ubiquitousness' does not amount to 'Another Declaration.'

† § †

४४. अत्यन्तासम्बद्धं चेदं - प्रतिज्ञां प्रतिज्ञासाधनायाहेति। यो हि प्राक् प्रतिज्ञामुक्त्वा हेतूदाहरणादिकं वक्तुं जानाति, स किञ्चिदनुक्रमं [कञ्चिदनुक्रमं?] साधनस्य जानात्येव हि। जानन् कथमविकलान्तःकरणः प्रतिज्ञामेव प्रतिज्ञासाधनायोपाददीत?

उपाददता चानेन प्रतिज्ञामात्रेण सिद्धिरिष्टा भवति। ततश्च न प्रागपि हेतुं ब्रूयात्।

एवंप्रकाराणामसम्बद्धानां परिसंख्यातुमशक्यत्वात् लक्षणनियमोऽप्यसम्बद्ध एव - प्रतिज्ञान्तराभिधाने प्रतिज्ञान्तरं नाम निग्रहस्थानमिति। एवम्प्रकाराणामेकमेव लक्षणं वाच्यं स्यात्।

न चैवंविधः कश्चिद् विवादेषु दृष्टपूर्वो व्यवहारो येन तदर्थं यत्नः क्रियते। न च बालप्रलापानुद्दिश्य शास्त्रं प्रवर्तते। प्रवृत्तौ च का निष्ठा, तेषामनिष्ठानात्?

44. Moreover, the statement that "One makes a (different) Declaration for proving the (earlier) Declaration," is totally irrelevant. The one who knows how to express the Declaration first and then probans, then instance etc., certainly knows the particular order in which the probans is to be presented. How in spite of knowing it and in spite of possessing an undivided mind, would he (= the disputant) employ a Declaration for proving a Declaration?

And if he does employ (one Declaration for proving another Declaration), then he desires that a thesis may be proved by mere Declaration! In that case he would not express probans previously (= in the first argument) also!

Such irrelevant type of cases being countless, to make a regulation by definition as "The occasion of defeat called 'Another Declaration' occurs when another Declaration is made (for proving one Declaration)" is also quite inappropriate. There should be stated only one such definition for covering (all) cases of this type.

Moreover, no such practice (of using one Declaration for proving another Declaration) has been observed in debates before, in the case of which one would make an attempt for covering it. A discipline (= *śāstra*) does not operate with reference to childish chatters and if it operates, then what status will it have? Because they (= childish chatters) do not have any status.

† § †

४५. दृश्यते च विदुषामपि नातिनिरूपणादसिद्धाभिधानमिति व्यवहारदर्शनात् तादृशं पराजयाधिकरणं व्यवस्थाप्यते। तस्मादिहापि यदि निवृत्ताकांक्षे वादिनि परोऽनैकान्तिकतामुद्भावयेद्, असाधनाङ्गस्यानैकान्तिकस्याभिधानान्निग्रहस्थानं वादिनः।

एवं यदि प्रतिवादी सत्सामान्यमैन्द्रियकं नित्यं च प्रमाणेन प्रतिपादयितुं शक्नुयात् अनुद्दिश्याप्रमाणकं शास्त्रोपगमं, प्रमाणेनैषामर्थानामप्रतिपादनेन भूतदोषोद्भावनमेतत्। न कश्चित्पराजयः, अभ्युपगममात्रेण वस्तुसिद्धेरभावात्, प्रतिवादिना दोषस्याप्रतिपादितत्वात्।

प्रमाणैरसमर्थितसाधनाभिधानात् तु जेताऽपि न भवतीति।

अनित्याकांक्षे [? अनिवृत्ताकांक्षे] पुनर्वादिनि न कश्चिद् दोषः, विशेषणाभिधानेन हेतोः समर्थनोपक्रमात्।

45. It is observed that even learned persons state Unproved probans because (sometimes) they do not see very clearly. When such practices are seen, the ground of

defeat is determined accordingly. Therefore, here also if the opponent points out the Inconclusiveness of probans when the disputant stops his inclination (to argue) it is the occasion of disputant's defeat because he (= the disputant) has stated a non-constituent of proof, namely, Inconclusive probans.

Thus if the opponent is able to state with evidence (= *pramāṇa*), without referring to a non-evident source from his discipline, that universal is real, knowable through senses and permanent, then, because he states these things with evidence, this amounts to pointing out the real fault in disputant's argument. No defeat is brought about merely by stating a hypothesis, because there is no proof of anything there. Also because, the fault (in disputant's argument) has not been pointed out by the opponent.

And because the disputant has stated a probans not justified by evidences, he does not become the winner also.

But if the disputant's inclination (to argue further) is not over then it is not any of his faults, because he may go on justifying himself by stating the qualifications of probans.

† § †

४६. [3.] "प्रतिज्ञाहेत्वोर्विरोध: प्रतिज्ञाविरोध:।" [न्या. सू. 5.2.4] यथा 'गुणव्यतिरिक्तं द्रव्यम्' इति प्रतिज्ञा, 'रूपादिभ्योऽर्थान्तरस्यानुपलब्धे:' इति हेतु:, सोऽयं प्रतिज्ञाहेत्वोर्विरोध:। एतेनैव प्रतिज्ञाविरोधोऽप्युक्त:, यत्र प्रतिज्ञा वचनेन [स्ववचनेन?][१] विरुध्यते। यथा – श्रमणा गर्भिणी, नास्त्यात्मेति वा।

हेतुविरोधोऽपि, यत्र प्रतिज्ञया हेतुर्विरुध्यते। यथा – 'सर्वं पृथक्, समूहे भावशब्दप्रयोगाद्' इति।

एतेन प्रतिज्ञया दृष्टान्तविरोधो व्याख्यात:।

---

१. (V); (?)

46. (3) [**Pratijñāvirodha** : Contrary Declaration]

"'Contrary Declaration' means the contrariety between Declaration and probans" (*N.S.* 5.2.4.)

[**Vātsyāyana explains:**] "For example the Declaration is, 'Substance is distinct from quality''; probans is, 'because no object other than colour etc. is apprehended.' This is the contrariety between Declaration and probans."

[**Udyotakara explains:**] "The 'Contrary Declaration' where Declaration is contradicted by the utterance (of the Declaration itself), is also implied by the above definition. For example, 'The nun is pregnant' or 'The self does not exist.'

"The 'Contrary probans', where the probans is contradicted by Declaration is also implied (by the same definition). For example, "Everything is discrete, because the term denoting a real is applicable to an aggregate only.

"This also explains the contrariety of instance to Declaration".

† § †

४७. हेतोश्च दृष्टान्तादिभिर्विरोधः, प्रमाणविरोधश्च [२]प्रतिज्ञाहेत्वोर्वक्तव्यः[२]।

यः परपक्षं स्वसिद्धेन गोत्वादिना व्यभिचारयति, तद् विरुद्धमुत्तरं वेदितव्यम्।

स्वपक्षानपेक्षं च। यं च स्वपक्षानपेक्षं हेतुं प्रयुङ्क्ते – 'अनित्यः शब्दः ऐन्द्रियकत्वाद्' इति, तस्य स्वसिद्धस्य गोत्वादेरनित्यविरोधाद् विरुद्धः। इति परपक्षेष्वसिद्धेन गोत्वादिनाऽनैकान्तिकचोदनाविरुद्धः।

उभयपक्षसम्प्रतिपन्नस्त्वनैकान्तिकः। यदुभयपक्षं [यदुभयपक्ष-?] प्रतिपन्नं वस्तु तेनानैकान्तिकचोदना इति।

---

२. In the light of NV 5.2.4; प्रतिज्ञाहेतोर्वक्तव्यः - (R), (V) and (D).

47. "One should also mention the contrariety of probans to instance etc. and contrariety of Declaration and probans to the means of knowledge.

"If one shows variability of relation, (between 'knowability through senses' and impermanence) in the other's argument, by referring to cowness etc. which is proved in one's own discipline, it is to be understood as a 'contrary reply.'[1] Same is the case where the probans is independent of one's own position.

"When one employes a probans irrespective of one's own position as 'Sound is impermanent, because knowable through senses', then that probans is contrary, because cowness etc. which is proved in (the disputant's) own discipline is contrary to impermanence. In this way if the 'Inconclusiveness' is pointed out with reference to the case of cowness etc., then it (= the probans) is contrary.

"But if it (= cowness etc.) is admitted by both the parties (that is, by disputant as well as opponent), then it is a case of Inconclusiveness. Because the claim of Inconclusiveness is based on something which is admitted by both the parties."

† § †

४८. अत्रापि प्रतिज्ञार्थः, साधनवाक्ये प्रयोगप्रतिषेधात्। तदाश्रयस्तत्कृतो वा हेतुदृष्टान्तयोर्न विरोध इति न प्रतिज्ञाविरोधो नाम किञ्चिन्निग्रहस्थानम्।

स्यादेतत्। असत्यपि प्रतिज्ञाप्रयोगे गम्यमानोऽपि प्रतिज्ञाहेत्वोर्विरोधो भवति। यथा – रूपादिभ्योऽर्थान्तरस्यानुपलब्धिस्तद् गुणव्यतिरिक्तम्, नोपलभ्यते च रूपादिभ्योऽर्थान्तरं द्रव्यम्। इत्युक्तेऽपि गम्यत एव साध्यसाधनयोर्विरोधः – कथं ततोऽर्थान्तरस्यानुपलब्धिः, तद्व्यतिरेकश्चेति।

सत्यं, स्यादयं विरोधः, यदि हेतुः साध्यधर्मविपर्ययं साधयेत्। यदि ह्युपलब्धिलक्षणव्यासत्वेन [ह्युपलब्धिलक्षणप्रासत्वेन ?] उपगतस्य सतो

द्रव्यरूपादिप्रतिभासविवेकेन स्वप्रतिभासानुपलब्धिस्तस्य तद्व्यतिरेके नास्ति [तद्व्यतिरेकेणास्ति ?] इति इष्टव्यतिरेक विपर्ययसाधनाद् विरुद्धो हेतुरस्माभिरुक्त एवेति। भवत्येवेदं निग्रहाधिकरणं, यद्येवंविध: प्रतिज्ञाहेतो: [? प्रतिज्ञाहेत्वो:] विरोध इष्ट:। अथ पुनरस्योपलब्धिलक्षणप्राप्तिर्लुप्यते, तदा न कश्चित् प्रतिज्ञाहेतो: [? प्रतिज्ञाहेत्वो:] विरोध:, व्यतिरिक्तानामपि भावानां कुतश्चिद् [3]विप्रकर्षिणां[3] तद्व्यतिरेकेणानुपलब्धावपि व्यतिरेकस्य भावात्।

48. [**Dharmakīrti's response**:] Here too (there is nothing like) the meaning of Declaration (which is supposed to be contrary to probans)! Because, employing Declaration in the inferential statement is prohibitted. So there is no contrariety between Declaration and probans which is grounded in it (= employment of Declaration) or generated by it. Therefore there is no occasion of defeat called 'Contrary Declaration.'

One might object, "Even if there is no employment of Declaration, the contrariety between Declaration and probans could be implied. For example (the inference may be stated as this;) "If any object apart from colour etc. is not apprehended, then that object is distinct from qualities; and a substance is not apprehended as an object apart from colour etc.".[1] Even if the argument is stated as this, the contrariety between probandum and probans is definitely understood, because how is it that there is non-apprehension of something other than that, and yet there exists the thing other than that?"

[**Answer**] True. This contrariety will be there if the probans proves the opposite of the probandum. Because, if the substance is known to be fulfilling the condition of apprehensibility and there is non-apprehension of the self-appearance of such a

---

३. (V); विप्रकर्षाणां - (R) and (D).

substance as distinct from the appearances of colour etc., then the probans will be contrary, as we have already said. Because, this probans proves the opposite of the intended (probandum, namely,) distinctness, (which is expressed as-) 'It (= substance) exists as distinct from it (= colour etc..)'. And it is definitely a ground of defeat if the contrariety of this kind between Declaration and probans is intended[2] (by you).

But if the fulfilment of the condition of apprehensibility by it (= the substance) is lost, then there is no contrariety between Declaration and probans, because then the distinctness of it (= substance) exists even if it is not apprehended because some distinct entities, which are remote in some respect[3], do exist distinctly (though they are not apprehended).

† § †

४९. यदुक्तं – 'स्ववचनप्रतिज्ञायाः [? प्रतिज्ञायाः] स्ववचनविरोधे प्रतिज्ञाविरोधः' इति तत्रेदमेव निग्रहाधिकरणम्, असाधनाङ्गभूतायाः प्रतिज्ञायाः साधनवाक्ये प्रयोगः, न विरोधः, तदधिकरणत्वात्।

यदि प्रतिज्ञानपेक्षो विरोधः स्यात्, स्यात् पराजयाश्रयः। प्रतिज्ञाधिकरणत्वे पुनस्तत्प्रयोगकृत एव पराजयः, अस्य प्रस्तावोपसंहारावसानत्वाद् व्यर्थं विरोधोद्भावनम्, पराजितपराजयाभावाद् भस्मीकृतानलवत्।

ये तु केचिद् विचारप्रसङ्गेषु एकत्र साध्ये बहवो हेतव उच्यन्ते, तेषां विकल्पेन तत्साध्यसाधनाय वृत्तेः सामर्थ्यम्, अन्यथा द्वितीयस्य वैयर्थ्यात्।

यदि हि तत्राप्येकप्रयोगमन्तरेणापरस्य प्रयोगो न सम्भवेत्, न तदा द्वितीयस्य कश्चित् साधनार्थः, प्रतीतप्रतिपादनाभावात्।

तस्मान्न प्रतिज्ञाया: स्ववचनविरोधो नाम किञ्चिन्निग्रहस्थानम्।

न च 'नास्त्यात्मा' इत्यत्र कश्चित् प्रतिज्ञाविरोध:, नास्त्यात्मशब्दार्थस्य भावोपादानत्वनिषेधात्। शब्दार्थनिषेधे हि विरोध: स्यात्। न च स्वलक्षणं शब्दार्थ इति।

49. On what you have said viz., "If Declaration uttered by oneself is contrary to it's own utterance, then it is a contrary Declaration," we say - That a Declaration, which is a non-constituent of proof, is employed in the inferential statement is itself a ground of defeat. This is not a case of contrariety, because that (= Declaration) itself is the ground.

If there is contrariety (between probans and probandum) independently of Declaration then it is a ground of defeat. But when Declaration is the ground of defeat, the defeat is due to employment of the Declaration itself. And because it [= Declaration] itself results into conclusion of the debate, it is futile to point out contrariety. Because, a defeated one is not defeated again, like fire which has turned into ashes (does not get extinguished again).[1]

We state many probans' for proving one (and the same) probandum on some occasions of discussions, but they have capasity to prove the probandum alternatively (i.e. independently of each other). Otherwise (i.e. if the second probans is not capable of proving the probandum independently of the first,) then the second probans will be superfluous.

If out of the two probans' (proving the same probandum), the employment of the other probans cannot be made without the employment of one, then (the probandum being proved by the first probans,) the second one has got nothing to prove, because what is already experienced is not to be established again.

Therefore there is no occasion of defeat called 'Contrariety of Declaration to its own utterance.'

Moreover, there is no 'contrariety of Declaration' in the statement 'Self does not exist'. Because it is denied that the meaning of the expression 'Self does not exist' corresponds to a real entity (= *bhāva*) (The expression does not deny that the word 'Self' has some meaning.) If the meaning of the word is denied then there will be (self) contrariety. Moreover, the meaning of a word is not the same as the self-characterised particular.[2]

† § †

५०. यः पुनः प्रतिज्ञाया बाधनाद्धेतुविरोध उक्तः, यथा – 'सर्वं पृथक् समूहे भावशब्दप्रयोगात्' इति। नात्र प्रतिज्ञाप्रयोगः, नापि हेतोः, येन विरोधः स्यात्। किं तर्हि? प्रतिपादितार्थोपदर्शनेनोपसंहारवचनमेतस्मात् [... वचनमेतत्स्यात्?]।

अन्यैरेव हेतुभिः शब्दस्यैकविशेषानभिधानम्, अनेकार्थसामान्याभिधानं च प्रतिपाद्य सर्वस्य शब्दार्थस्य नानार्थरूपतयैकवस्तुविशेषस्वभावताऽभावमुपदर्शयन् शब्दार्थमधिकृत्य सर्वं पृथगिति ब्रूयात्।

एतेन तद्विरोधः प्रत्युक्तः।

50. You have also talked of 'contrariety of probans (to Declaration) based on falsification of Declaration' as in 'Everything is discrete because the term denoting a real is applicable to an aggregate'. (Our view about this example is:) Here there is no employment of Declaration nor that of probans with which Declaration will have contrariety. What is there then? This would be the summing-up statement which presents the object (already) argued out. (This would happen as follows:) One first establishes by employing other reasons that the word (such as 'pot') does not express a single peculiar characteristic but expresses a common characteristic belonging to many objects. One then shows

that any meaning of a word is not by nature a single peculiar characteristic of a thing, as it is of the form of plurality of objects. Having shown this one may say, "Everything is discrete" with reference to the meaning of a word.

This answers the (accused) contrariety in this.

† § †

५१. दृष्टान्तोपदर्शनं चैतद् – 'अनित्यः शब्दः कृतकानित्यत्वाद्'।

यथा क्वचिद् अर्थे विप्रतिपत्तौ प्रसिद्धमनेकार्थसामान्ये शब्दप्रयोगमुपदर्श्य प्रतिपादितविप्रतिपत्तिस्थानः सामान्येनोपसंहरति – सर्वं पृथगिति।

यदि दृष्टान्तप्रयोगः, किमृजुनैव तत्प्रयोगक्रमेण न प्रयुक्तः, विप्रतिपत्तिविषयश्च किं न दर्शित इति चेत्।

न, समासनिर्देशात्। एवमपि प्रयोगदर्शनाद्, असाधनवाक्यत्वाच्च।

अत एव न प्रतिज्ञया हेतोर्बाधनम्। न चैकमेव किञ्चिन्नास्तीति ब्रुवाणः कश्चित् तत्समुच्चयरूपमेकं च समूहमिच्छति, येन विरोधः स्यात्।

योऽपि 'युगपत् पङ्क्तेन योगाद्' इत्यादिना परमाणोर्भेदमाह, न तस्याप्येकः समुच्चयरूपः साधयितुमिष्टः। किं तर्हि? अभाव एव, एकानेकप्रतिषेधात्। अतः सोऽपि न समूहस्तस्येष्टो न तत्र शब्द इति न विरोधः।

51. **[Alternative explanation:]** Moreover, the statement (viz. Everything is discrete because a term denoting a real is applicable to an aggregate only) could be taken as an indication of the instance, just as 'Sound in impermanent, because products are impermanent' (is a statement indicating the instance).[1] For example when there is dispute on some matter, the disputant shows that a word is admittedly used for a common property covering many objects and having argued for the disputed point, concludes in general, 'Everything is discrete'.

[A possible objection:] "If it amounts to employment of instance, why is the instance not employed in its straight mode of employment? And why is not the object of dispute indicated in that way?"

[Answer] No, because it is shown in an abridged form. We see the uses (of argument) in this form also. Secondly the statement under consideration is not the statement of proof (but it only resembles the proof).[2]

For the same reason there is no falsification of probans by the Declaration here. Here one (i.e. the Buddhist) is not intending to accept some collection which is composite in nature and (yet) is singular, when one says that there is nothing such as a single object. If one accepts it (= a collection which is composite and yet singular) then there would be contrariety.

Even the one who talks of the particularity (= *bheda*) of atom by saying, 'Since there is conjunction (of atoms) with the mud at once' etc.,[3] does not intend to prove a single object of composite nature. What then? He intends to prove the absence of such an object because manyness of one thing is denied. Therefore in that inference, the object intended to be proved is not a collection and a word is not made applicable to it. Therefore there is no contrariety (between Declaration and probans here).

† § †

५२. न विरुद्धोऽयं पूर्वकात् प्रतिज्ञाहेतुविरोधात् भिद्यते, येन पृथगुच्येत।

तत्र हेतुप्रतिज्ञयोर्बाधनम्, इह प्रतिज्ञया हेतोरित्यस्ति भेद इति चेत्। अर्थविरोधे हि हेतुप्रतिज्ञयोर्बाध्यबाधकभावः स्यात्। 'सर्वार्थविरोधो द्विषु' इति यमपि

[यदपि?] परस्परं बाधकम्, एकार्थसन्निधावपरार्थासम्भवात्, तत्र हेतुप्रतिज्ञयो: [३]सह पृथग्वा[३] बाधोदाहरणयोर्न कश्चिदर्थभेद:।

52. Secondly, this case of contrariety[1] does not differ from the earlier contrariety, in which case (i.e. in case it differs) it would be mentioned separately.

[A possible Nyāya objection:] "There,(= in the earlier case) there was falsification of probans and Declaration (by some evidence) but here there is falsification of probans by the Declaration. So there is a difference."

[Answer:] There will be the relation of falsified-and-falsifier between probans and Declaration if they are contrary to objects (= facts). Following the principle, "If there is contrariety between two things then the two things are contrary to all objects", if any thing (= any pair) is mutually falsifying, because if one object is accepted, the other object becomes impossible, then there is no substantial difference between the two examples of contrariety - whether it is collective contrariety (of probans and Declaration to some evidences) or a separate contrariety (of Declaration and probans to each other).

† § †

५३. अपि चायं विरुद्धो वा सति हेतुप्रयोगे व्यधिकरणत्वादसिद्ध इत्यसिद्धता हेतोर्निग्रहस्थानम्। स खलूच्यमान एवातद्धर्मतया प्रतीतो वक्तु: पराजयमानयति। पराजिते तस्मिंस्तदर्थविरोधचिन्तया न किञ्चित्।

अपि च - सर्वत्रायं प्रतिज्ञाहेत्वोर्विरोध: सम्भवन् द्वयीं दोषजातिमभिपतति विरुद्धतामसिद्धतां चेति।

३. As an alternative reading accepted in V; पृथग् - (R) and (D).

विरुद्धता सिद्धे हेतोर्धर्मिणि भावे साध्यधर्मविपर्यय एव, भाव प्रतिज्ञाविरोधात्।

असिद्धता पुनर्धर्मिणि प्रतिज्ञातार्थसिद्धौ, विरुद्धयोः स्वभावयोः एकत्रासम्भवात्, न चान्यथा विरोधः।

असिद्धे धर्मस्वभावेऽभिहितयोर्हेतुप्रतिज्ञातार्थयोर्विरोधाद् विरोधसम्भव इति चेत्।

अप्रमाणयोगे तूभयोर्धर्मिणि संशयः। तथा सति हेतोर्धर्मिणि भावसंशयेऽसिद्धतैव हेतुदोष इत्यसिद्धविरुद्धाभ्यामन्यो न प्रतिज्ञया विरोधो नाम पराजयहेतुः।

असिद्धविरुद्धे च हेत्वाभासवचनादेवोक्ते इति न पृथक् प्रतिज्ञाविरोधो वक्तव्य इति।

53. Moreover, is it (= the inference, "Everything is discrete because a term denoting a real is applicable to an aggregate only") a case of Contrary probans or it is an Unproved probans because it has a different substratum (from that of probandum) (and this is noticed) as soon as there is employment of probans and hence Unproveness of probans is the occasion of defeat here? Because, (i.e., latter is the case, because) this kind of (Unproved) probans, as soon as it is uttered, is recognised as not being the property of that (= the bearer of the probandum) and brings about the defeat of the speaker. When the speaker is defeated, the concern whether the object of it (= probans) is contrary (to Declaration) has no significance.

Moreover, in every case this contrariety between Declaration and probans, when it occurs, falls into two types of faults: Contrariety and Unprovedness.

Contrariety is nothing but the absence of probandum - property, when the existence of probans in the property-bearer (= locus) is proved, because existence of (such a) probans is contrary to Declaration.

Unprovedness on the other hand takes place when the declared object (= probandum) is proved (by some other means) in the property-bearer (= locus) (and the probans being contrary to probandum is non-existent in the property-bearer) because two contrary natures cannot exist in one place; otherwise there is no contrariety.[1]

[A possible Nyāya objection:] "Contrariety (of Declaration) is possible even when the nature of the (probans -) property is unproved because there would be contrariety between the expressed probans and the declared object."

[Answer] When the evidence is not available to both (disputant as well as opponent) there arises doubt about (the existence of probans in) the property-bearer. In that case, when there is doubt about the existence of probans in the property-bearer, Unprovedness is the only fault in probans. Therefore there is no cause of defeat called 'Contrariety of Declaration' apart from (the fallacies of probans called) Unproved and Contrary probans.

And Unproved and Contrary probans are covered by the mention of 'fallacies of probans' (as one of the occasions of defeat). Therefore 'Contrary Declaration' should not be stated separately (as an occasion of defeat).

† § †

५४. उभयाश्रयत्वाद् विरोधस्य विवक्षातोऽन्यतरनिर्देश इति चेत्। स्यादेतत्। प्रतिज्ञाहेत्वोर्विरोध इति प्रतिज्ञाहेतू आश्रित्योभयाश्रयो भवति। तत्र यदा

प्रतिज्ञाविरोधो विवक्षितस्तदा प्रतिज्ञाविरोध इत्युच्यते, यदा प्रतिज्ञाया हेतोर्वा विरोधस्तदा विरुद्धो हेतुरिति। अतः प्रतिज्ञाविरोधः, हेतुविरोधो वा इत्यदोषः।

तत्र हेतोरुदाहरणम् – नित्यः शब्दः उत्पत्तिधर्मकत्वादिति। प्रतिज्ञाविरोधस्य – नास्त्यात्मेति। प्रतिज्ञाहेत्वोः परस्परविरुद्धोदाहरणम् – गुणव्यतिरिक्तमित्यादि। प्रतिज्ञया हेतुविरोधोदाहरणम् 'नास्त्येको भाव' इत्यादिकम् इति। न, सर्वहेत्वपेक्षस्य विरोधहेत्वाभासानतिक्रमात्, यथोक्तं प्राक्।

अनपेक्षे च केवले स्वतः प्रतिविरोधे [प्रतिज्ञाविरोधे?] विवक्षिते प्रतिज्ञाहेत्वोर्विरोध इति हेतुग्रहणमसम्बद्धम्।

न चोत्पत्तिधर्मत्वान्नित्यमित्यत्रापि हेतुविरोधो युक्तः। प्रतिज्ञया हि हेतोर्बाधने हेतुविरोधः, इह तु हेतुना प्रतिज्ञा बाध्यते इति प्रतिज्ञाविरोधो युक्तः।

उभयाश्रयेऽपि विरोधे बाध्यमानविवक्षया तद्विरोधव्यवस्थापनात्।

54. **[A possible objection:]** "Since contrariety (always) holds between two objects, any one of them could be mentioned by the speaker according to his intention".

[Answer] That is possible. (You might say:) The contrariety of Declaration and probans holds between Declaration and probans. So it is dependent on two relata. So it is called 'Contrariety of Declaration', when the contrariety of Declaration is intended and it is called 'Contrary probans' when contrariety of probans to Declaration is intended. Therefore there is no fault in calling it either 'Contrariety of Declaration' or 'Contrariety of probans.'

The example of (contrary) probans is - 'Sound is permanent because it is subject to generation'. The example of contrariety of Declaration is- 'There is no Self'. The example of mutual contrariety between Declaration and probans is 'Substance is distinct from quality etc.'[1] The example of contrariety of probans to Declaration is, 'There is no single object' etc.[2]

(Although you might say this, our comment here is twofold-) You cannot say so (i.e., you cannot treat them as different types of 'Contrary Declaration') Because, as we said here before, no case of contrariety dependent on probans falls outside the scope of the fallacy of contrary probans.

And if it is intended that there is contrariety in the Declaration itself, in isolation, (i.e.,) independently (of probans) then employment of the term 'probans' in (the definition of Contrary Declaration as-) 'Contrariety between Declaration and probans' would be irrelevant.

Moreover, it is not proper to say that there is 'contrariety to probans' (= *hetuvirodhaḥ*) in example, "Sound is permanent because it is subject to generation", because there wiil be 'contrariety to probans' (properly so called) when the Declaration falsifies probans. But here the probans falsifies the Declaration. It is therefore proper to call this example as that of 'contrariety to Declaration'.

Because, although contrariety holds between two objects, that to which there is contrariety is determined relative to what is falsified.

† § †

५५. यदप्युक्तम् - एतेन प्रतिज्ञया दृष्टान्तविरोधादयोऽपि वक्तव्या भण्डालेख्यन्यायेनेति, तत्रापि पक्षीकृतधर्मविपर्ययवति दृष्टान्ते विरोधः स्यात्। विरुद्धे च दृष्टान्ते यदि पक्षधर्मस्य वृत्तिरनन्यसाधारणा प्रसाध्यते, विरुद्धस्तदा हेत्वाभासः।

साधारणायामप्रसाधिते वा तद्वृत्तिनियमेऽनैकान्तिकः। अवृत्तौ ४वाऽसाधारणः४।

विरुद्धदृष्टान्तावृत्तौ विपर्ययवृत्तौ च न कश्चिद् हेतुदोषः, दृष्टान्तविरोधश्च प्रतिज्ञाया इति चेत्।

न, तदापि संशयहेतुत्वानतिवृत्तेः। दृष्टान्तविरोधो हि प्रतिज्ञायाः साधर्म्ये दोषो न वैधर्म्ये, अभिमतत्वात्।

साधर्म्यदृष्टान्ते च विपरीतधर्मवति वस्तुतः साध्याव्यभिचारेऽपि हेतोर्नाव्यभिचारधर्मता शक्या दर्शयितुमिति नाप्रदर्शिताविनाभावसम्बन्धात् हेतोर्निश्चयः। तत्र ५प्रतिज्ञया५ दृष्टान्तविरोधो हेत्वाभासानतिवर्तते।

55. You (= Udyotakara) have said by following the allegorical principle viz., 'the picture drawn by a buffoon',[1] "By this (definition of contrary Declaration,) the contrariety of Declaration to instance etc. should also be said (to be covered)" We say on this - There will be contrariety of instance if the instance possesses the absence of the provable property.[2] If the existence of probans is proved to be there in such a contrary instance exclusively, then it is a case of the fallacy of probans, viz. Contrary probans.[3]

But if the existence of probans is common (to contrary instances as well as other instances), or if the rule about its existence is unproved, then it is a case of the fallacy of probans called Inconclusive. Or if proban does not exist (both in positive contrary instances as well as other instances) then it is a case of the fallacy of probans called Uncommon.

[A possible Nyāya objection:] "A probans does not exist in the contrary instance but exists in the opposite instances,[4]

४. (V); वा साधारणः - (R) and (D).

५. (R); प्रतिज्ञाया - (V) and (D).

then there is no fault in probans, but the Declaration does have contrariety to instance."

[Answer] No. Because, (in the case cited by you) the probans does not exceed dubitability. Because, the contrariety of Declaration to the instance[5] is a fault when it is with regard to positive instance, not when it is with regard to negative instance, because such a contrariety (i.e. the one with regard to negative instance) is desirable.

When the positive instance possesses a property contrary (to probandum), although probans in fact has invariable relation with probandum, the invariable character of the probans cannot be demonstrated (because the positive instance is defective) and there cannot be determinate cognition (of the probandum) caused by the probans unless its relation of invariable concomitance (with the probandum) is demonstrated. Therefore the contrariety of Declaration to instance does not fall outside the fallacies of probans.

† § †

५६. उभयथाऽपि दोषोऽस्त्विति चेत्। न। न हेतुदोषस्य प्राक् 'प्रसङ्गेन'[६] पराजितस्य दोषान्तरानपेक्षणात्।

विशेषेण साधनावयवानुक्रमनियमवादिनः। उदाहरणसाधर्म्यं हेतुलक्षणं विरुद्धे दृष्टान्ते न सम्भवतीति प्राक्प्रयुक्तस्य हेतोर्दोषेण पराजय इति नोत्तरदृष्टान्तापेक्षया विरोधश्चिन्तामर्हति।

हेतोरपि दृष्टान्तविरोधेऽसाधारणत्वं विरुद्धत्वं वा, वैधर्म्ये यदि वृत्तिः स्यात्।

---

६. (V); प्रसङ्गो न – (R) and (D).

प्रमाणविरोधे तु हेतोर्यथा - 'न दहनोऽग्निः शैत्यात्' इत्यादि ह्यसिद्धो हेत्वाभासः।

प्रतिज्ञायाः प्रमाणविरोधः स्ववचनविरोधेन व्याख्यातः। इति सर्वे एवैते साधनविरोधे हेत्वाभासेष्वन्तर्भवन्तीति हेत्वाभासवचनेनैवोक्ताः।

56. [**A Naiyāyika might say:**] "Let there be fault in both ways".

[**Answer**] No. Because, the fault in probans has prior occurrence. And it is not expected to discover another fault, once the disputant is defeated (due to the fault in probans).

This is true especially in the case of one who insists on the rule regarding the order of the elements of proof.[1] The defining characteristic of probans viz. 'similarity with (positive) instance' becomes inapplicable to the probans if the (positive) instance is contrary. Hence the defeat of the disputant takes place due to the fault in probans which is employed before (instance).

Hence the contrariety (of Declaration) with respect to instance, which is employed later, does not deserve our concern.

If probans has contrariety to (positive) instance (i.e. it does not exist in the positive instance) then there will be (the fallacy of probans called) Uncommon. Or if the probans (that does not exist in positive instances) exists in the negative instance then there will be (the fallacy of probans called) Contrariety.

On the other hand when probans is contrary to a means of knowledge, like in the example, "Fire does not burn because it is cold," there is the fallacy called Unproved probans.

'The contrariety of Declaration to a means of knowledge' is explained (i.e. examined) through (the examination of) 'Contrariety to its own utterence.'

In this way all these cases are included in the fallacies of probans when there is contrariety in the proof.

† § †

५७. यत्तु विरुद्धमुत्तरं परपक्षे स्वसिद्धेन गोत्वादिनानैकान्तिकचोदनेति, तदसम्बद्धमेव। यदि हि स्वसिद्धेन गोत्वादिना परस्य व्यभिचारसिद्धिमाकाङ्क्षेत, तस्य तत्स्वपक्षविरुद्धं नाभिमतमिति विरोधो युज्येत। स हि स्वयं प्रतिपन्ने गोत्वे हेतुवृत्तेः संशयानोऽप्रतिपत्तिमात्मनस्तथा ख्यापयति।

स च हेतुः सत्यसति गोत्वेऽप्रसाधितसाधनसामर्थ्यः संशये हेतुत्वाद-नैकान्तिक एव।

प्रसाधिते तु सामर्थ्ये गोत्वेऽवृत्त्या हेतौ न संशय एव, सर्वसंशयप्रकाराणां परिहारेण समर्थनात्।

एतेन स्वपक्षानपेक्षहेतुप्रयोगस्यानैकान्तिकता व्याख्याता। सोऽपि स्वाभिमतनित्यगोत्ववृत्तिहेतुमनित्यत्वे ब्रुवाणोऽसमर्थतयाऽसाधनाङ्गतया संशयहेतुमेवाहेति।

यत्पुनरुक्तम् – उभयपक्षसम्प्रतिपन्नेन वस्तुनाऽनैकान्तिकचोदनेति, तत्राप्यवश्यं संशयहेतुत्वमुखेनैवानैकान्तिको वक्तव्यः। तदसमर्थितेऽन्यत्रापि तुल्यमिति नोभयसिद्धेतरयोरनैकान्तिकत्वविशेषः।

57. But your statement viz. "Accusing the other's argument of the fallacy of Inconclusive probans, by referring to 'cowness',[1] which is proved in one's own discipline, amounts to contrary reply," is quite irrelevant (to the occasion of defeat called contrary Declaration).

Because, if the opponent claims to prove the variability of relation (between probans and probandum) by referring to cowness etc., which is proved in his own discipline, then the contrariety (of his reply) will be right, because the cowness etc. which is contrary to the disputant's own position is not accepted by him (=disputant). Because, he (=the opponent) doubts the existence of the probans in cowness, which is accepted by himself, and hence exhibits his own lack of understanding.

But whether cowness exists or not, the probans remains Inconclusive, when its capasity to prove (the probandum) is not established, because it causes doubt.

If on the other hand its capasity (to prove the probandum) is established, then in that case it does not exist in cowness and hence there is no doubt regarding the probans at all, because it (= capasity of probans) is established by removing all sorts of doubts.[2]

This also explains the inconclusiveness of the probans which is employed independently of one's own position. Such an employment of probans also amounts to applying the probans that exists in the permanent 'cowness' accepted by oneself, for proving impermanence. Hence such an employment of probans being incapable (of proving probandum) amounts to employing dubitable probans only, as it is a non-constituent of proof.

You also said, "There is (sometimes) a claim of inconclusiveness on the basis of something which is admitted by both the parties". Here also one should talk of inconclusiveness necessarily based on the probans causing doubt. This factor (namely the probans causing doubt) is common to other cases (of inconclusiveness) also, hence there is no difference between the inconclusiveness in this case where something is admitted by both the parties, and the one in other cases.

५८. यदप्युक्तं - 'दृष्टान्ताभासा हेत्वाभासपूर्वकत्वात् तदभिधानेनैवोक्ता इति न पृथग् निग्रहस्थानेषूक्ताः' इति तदप्यवयवान्तरवादिनोऽयुक्तम्। योऽवयवान्तरं दृष्टान्तहेतोः [दृष्टान्तं हेतोः?] आह, तस्य न हेत्वाभासोक्त्या दृष्टान्ताभासोक्तिर्व्याप्या, तद्वचनेन गम्यमानस्य तस्मात् साधनान्तराभावप्रसङ्गात्।

दृष्टान्ताभासानां हेत्वाभासेऽप्यन्तर्भावाद् दृष्टान्तस्यापि हेतावन्तर्भाव इष्टो भवति। "तथा" च न दृष्टान्तः पृथक्साधनावयवः स्याद्, अपृथग्वृत्तेः।

यो दृष्टान्तसाध्योऽर्थस्तस्य हेतावन्तर्भावाद्धेतुनैव साधित इति न दृष्टान्तस्य पृथक् किञ्चित्सामर्थ्यम्।

अपि च - न किञ्चित् पूर्वपक्षवादिनो हेत्वाभासासंस्पर्शे न्याय्यं निग्रहस्थानमस्तीति तत्सम्बन्धीनि सर्वाण्येव हेत्वाभासतावचनेनैव उक्तानीति न पृथग्वाच्यानि स्युः।

अर्थान्तरगमनादेरपि हेतोरसामर्थ्ये एव सम्भवात्। न हि समर्थे हेतौ साध्ये च सिद्धेऽर्थान्तरगमनं कश्चिदारभते, असमर्थस्य मिथ्याप्रवृत्तेरिति।

58. You also said, "Because the fallacies of instance arise out of the fallacies of probans, so the former are covered by the mention of the latter. Therefore the former are not mentioned separately in the list of the occasions of defeat." This too cannot be held rightfully by the advocates of (instance as) a distinct element in the argument.

The mention of the fallacies of probans cannot cover the mention of the fallacies of instance according to the one who talks of instance as an element distinct from probans. Because, if it (= a fallacy of instance) is covered by the mention of them (= fallacies of probans) then it (= instance) will not be a distinct constituent of proof from that (= probans).

---

७. (R); तत्र - (V) and (D).

If the fallacies of instance are included in the fallacies of probans, then it is desirable also to include instance in the probans. In that case instance will not be a separate element of proof, as it does not have separate existence.

The object which is to be proved by the instance is included in the (object to be proved by) probans. Therefore it is proved by probans only and hence the instance has no power separately.

Moreover, any occasion of defeat of the disputant (= the defender of the first position; *pūrvapakṣavādin*) is not justly so if it is not connected with a fallacy of probans. Hence all the cases (of occasions of defeat) related with it (= a fallacy of probans) are covered by the mention of 'fallacies of probans' (in the list of the occasions of defeat) and hence they do not deserve a separate mention.

Because, the occasion of defeat such as 'Shifting to a different point' is also possible only when the probans is incapable (of proving the probandum). Because, r body begins to shift to a different point if the probans (employed by him) is sound and the probandum is proved. Because, only an incapable person goes for false practices.

† § †

५९. [४.] "पक्षप्रतिषेधे प्रतिज्ञातार्थापनयनं प्रतिज्ञासंन्यासः।" [न्या. सू. ५.२.५] यं प्रतिज्ञातमर्थम् 'अनित्यः शब्दः ऐन्द्रियकत्वाद्' इति सामान्यवृत्त्या हेतोर्व्यभिचारप्रदर्शनेन सः प्रतिषेधे कृते, 'क एवमाह–अनित्यः शब्दः' इति परित्यजति, तस्य प्रतिज्ञासंन्यासो नाम निग्रहस्थानमिति।

अत्रापि यद्युद्भाविते ऽपि हेतोर्व्यभिचारे न सपक्षं [स्वपक्षं परित्यजति?], किं न गृह्येत? अनिगृह त [? अनिगृहीत] एव हेत्वाभासाभिधानादिति चेत्।

किमिदानीमुत्तरप्रतिज्ञासंन्यासापेक्षया तस्य तदेवाद्यं निग्रहस्थानमिति किमन्यैरशक्तपरिच्छेदैः क्लीबप्रलापप्रचेष्टितैरुपन्यस्तैः? एवं हि अतिप्रसङ्गः

स्यात्। पक्षप्रतिषेधे तूष्णीम्भवतस्तूष्णीम्भावो नाम निग्रहस्थानम्, प्रपलायमानस्य प्रपलायितं नामेति एवमाद्यपि वाच्यं स्यात्। तस्मादेतदपि असम्बद्धमिति।

59. (4) [**Pratijñāsaṁnyāsa:** Renunciation of Declaration]

"'Renunciation of Declaration' means removing (i.e. disowning) the declared thesis when one's position is repudiated (by the opponent)" (*NS* 5.2.5.)

[Nyāya explanation:] "The disputant first declares the thesis as 'Sound is impermanent because it is knowable through senses' and when it is repudiated by showing the variability of relation of the probans (with the probandum) by referring to the existence of the probans in universals, he disowns the thesis by saying, "Who said that the sound is impermanent?" It is an occasion of his defeat, called 'Renunciation of Declaration'."

[Dharmakīrti's response:] If in this case the disputant does not disown his own position, then will he not be defeated?

If you say, "(He will not be defeated) because here the disputant expresses fallacious probans when he is not defeated (i.e. not caught by the opponent),"[1] then we ask.-

What is the point in looking forward to the later renunciation of Declaration? The earlier event (of one's argument being repudiated by the opponent) is itself the occasion of one's (= disputant's) defeat. What is the use of introducing the other innumerable acts of impotent chatter (as the varieties of occasion of defeat)? In this way there will be transgression (of reason). Becoming silent when one's position is repudiated will be an occasion of defeat called 'Becoming silent'; if one runs away (when one's position is repudiated), then it will be an occasion of defeat called 'Running away'. The occasions of defeat such as these will all have to be mentioned (separately). Therefore this (occasion of defeat) is also irrelevant.

६०. [५.] "अविशेषोक्ते हेतौ प्रतिषिद्धे विशेषमिच्छतो हेत्वन्तरम्।" [न्या.सू.५.२.६.] निदर्शनम् – 'एकप्रकृतीदं व्यक्तं, 'परिमाणात्', मृत्पूर्वकाणां शरावप्रभृतीनां दृष्टं परिमाणम्' इति।

अस्य व्यभिचारेण प्रत्यवस्थानम् - नानाप्रकृतीनामेकप्रकृतीनां च दृष्टं परिमाणमिति।

एवं प्रत्यवस्थित आह - एकप्रकृतिसमन्वयप्रकाराणां परिणामदर्शनात् [परिमाणदर्शनात्?]। सुखदुःखमोहसमन्वितं हीदं सर्वं व्यक्तं परिगृह्यते [परिमितं गृह्यते?][८]। तस्य प्रकृत्यन्तररूपसमन्वयाभावोऽसति [? प्रकृत्यन्तररूपसमन्वयाभावे सति] एकप्रकृतिकत्वमिति तदविशेषोक्ते हेतौ प्रतिषेधं ब्रुवतो हेत्वन्तरं भवति। सति हेत्वन्तरभावे पूर्वस्य हेतोरसाधकत्वान्निग्रहस्थानम्।

अत्रापि पूर्वस्यैव हेतोरनैकान्तिकस्याभिधानान्निगृहीते हेत्वन्तरचिन्ता क्वोपयुज्यते? यदि प्राक्साधनवादी हेतुमनैकान्तिकमुक्त्वा दत्तोत्तरावसरः तेनैव निगृह्यते। अदत्तोत्तरावसरो हेत्वन्तराभिधानेऽपि न निग्रहमर्हति, अविरामात्।

60. (5) [**Hetvantara**: Another probans]

"'Another probans' occurs when one desires to present the qualified probans when the probans stated without qualifications is repudiated". (*NS* 5.2.6.)

[**Vātsyāyana explains-**] "For example, "The manifest has singular original nature (= *prakṛti*) because it has a limited size (= *parimāṇa*). For instance it is seen that the things like (earthen) plate etc. which are produced from (a single substance viz.) mud, have limited size."

"This argument is repudiated (by the opponent) by pointing out the variability (of the relation) in the following way - "The things having manifold original nature as also the things having singular (i.e. common) original nature are seen to have limited size."

---

८. (V); परिणामात् - (R) and (D)

९. Supported bv V

"When repudiated in this way, the disputant says: (We state our probans as follows:) "Because 'limited size' is observed in the kinds of objects co-ordinated by a singular original nature[1]; and all these manifest objects which are co-ordinated by pleasure, pain and delusion, are known to have limited size; (hence) they have a singular original nature and the lack of co-ordination with any other original nature." In this way it becomes a case of Another probans when someone repudiates the unqualified probans.

"When another probans is presented the earlier probans proves to be incapable of proving (the probandum) and hence an occasion of defeat."

[Dharmakīrti's response:] In this too, where is the point in thinking about the other probans, as the disputant is already defeated due to the earlier statement of the Inconclusive probans? If the proposer of the first probans expresses an Inconclusive probans and is given an opportunity to respond (to the objections) then he gets defeated due to the same (Inconclusive probans). But if he is not given an opportunity to respond (to the objections) then even if he presents another probans, he is not worthy of being defeated, because there is no closure (of the debate in that case).

† § †

६१. [६.] "प्रकृतादर्थादप्रतिबद्धार्थमर्थान्तरम्" [न्या. सू. ५.२.७.] यथोक्तलक्षणे पक्षप्रतिपक्षपरिग्रहे हेतुतः साध्यसिद्धौ प्रकृतायां कुर्यात्-नित्यः शब्दोऽस्पर्शत्वादिति हेतुः। हेतुश्च नाम हिनोतेर्धातोस्तुशब्दे प्रत्यये कृदन्तं पदम्। पदं च नामाख्यातोपसर्गनिपाता इति प्रस्तुत्य नामादीनि व्याचष्टे। इदमर्थान्तरं नाम निग्रहस्थानम्, अभ्युपगतार्थासङ्गतत्वादिति।

न्याय्यमेतन्निग्रहस्थानं, पूर्वोत्तरपक्षवादिनोः प्रतिपादिते दोषे प्रकृतं परित्यज्यासाधनाङ्गवचनमदोषोद्भावनं च। साधनवादिना ह्युपन्यस्तसाधनस्य समर्थने

कर्तव्ये तदकृत्वा परस्य प्रसङ्गेनाप्रसङ्गेन वाऽतन्नान्तरीयकस्याभिधान-मुत्तरवादिनोऽपि दोषोद्भावनमात्रादपरस्योपक्षेप इति।

61. (6) [**Arthāntara:** Different point]

"'Different point' means (speaking) something, the content of which is irrelevant to the topic under consideration". (*NS* 5.2.7.)

[**Vātsyāyana explains:**] "When the position and the counter-position are held in accordance with their definitions (by disputant and opponent respectively) and proof of the probandum on the basis of probans is due, one (= the disputant) would say, "Sound is permanent. The *hetu* (= probans) is - 'because intangible'. 'Hetu' is a word ending with *kṛt* - suffix when the word *tu* is attached as suffix to the root '*hi*' (= '*hinoti*'). Words are of four kinds - noun, verb, prefix and particle." Having initiated (a different point) in this way he explains noun etc."

[**Udyotkara explains:**] "This is an occasion of defeat called 'Different point', because here the disputant's speech is irrelevant to the proposed topic."

[**Dharmakīrti's response:**] This occasion of defeat is legitimate one. It amounts to first leaving the issue at hand when the fault (in one's argument) is pointed out (by the other debater) and then 'stating a non-constituent of proof' or 'pointing out a non-fault', on the parts of disputant and opponent respectively. Because, when the proposer of the argument is required to give justification of his proposed argument, he states instead of that something that is not invariably connected with the proposed topic either by relating it to the context or not. And from the side of the respondent (i.e. opponent) it amounts to expressing something other than discovery of the fault (of the disputant).

६२. [७.] ''वर्णक्रमनिर्देशवन्निरर्थकम्।'' [न्या. सू. ५.२.८] यथा 'नित्यः शब्दो जबगडत्वात् झभघढवद्' इति। 'साधनानुपादानात्'[१] निगृह्यते इति।

इदमप्यसम्बद्धम्। न हि वर्णक्रमनिर्देशसिद्धावानर्थक्यं यदेव किञ्चिद-साधनाङ्गस्य वचनं तदेवानर्थकं; साध्यसिद्ध्युपयोगिनोऽभिधेयस्याभावात्, निष्प्रयोजनत्वाच्चेति। प्रकारविशेषोपादानमसम्बद्धम्।

वतेरुपादानाददोष इति चेत्। स्यादेतत्: वर्णक्रमनिर्देशवदिति वतिरत्रोपात्तः सोऽन्यदापि [सोऽन्यदपि?] अननुरूपं गृह्णाति इत्यदोषः इति।

न। अर्थान्तरादेर्निग्रहस्थानस्यावचनप्रसङ्गात्। एवं हि ता निरर्थका वाच्या निरर्थकेनैवाभिधानाहितम् [निरर्थकेनैवाभिधानात्?]।

न साध्यसिद्धौ अनर्थकं निरर्थकं, यस्य नैव कश्चिदर्थस्तन्निरर्थकमिष्टमिति चेत्।

यस्य कस्यचिदवादिनोऽपि हि निरर्थकाभिधाने किं न निग्रहः? निग्रह-निमित्ताविशेषात्।

न; तस्येहाप्रस्तावादिति चेत्।

आयातमिह - यो निरर्थकं ब्रवीति, तस्य तेनैव निग्रह इति। तत्तुल्यं सर्वस्यासाधनाङ्गवादिन इति। स सर्वो निरर्थकाभिधानोऽप्यनेनैव निग्रहस्थानेन निग्रहार्हः।

न च वर्णक्रमनिर्देशः सर्वत्र निरर्थकः; क्वचित्प्रकरणे तस्याप्यर्थवत्त्वात्। तस्मादत्रैवास्यानर्थक्यात् निग्रहस्थानत्वम्। अपि चान्यदिदमुच्यते - 'वर्णक्रमनिर्देशो निग्रहस्थानम्' इति; कपोलवादितकंक्ष्यघट्टितकमित्येवमादीनामपि वाच्यत्वात्।

62. (7) [**Nirarthaka :** Meaningless utterance]

"'Meaningless utterance' means an act like uttering a series of letters." (*NS* 5.2.8.)

---

१. In the light of *NV* 5.2.8; साधनान्युपादानात् - (R) and (D).

[Vātsyāyana explains:] "For example, "Sound is permanent because (it is) *ja, ba, ga, ḍa,* like *jha, bha, gha, ḍha.*".

[Udyotakara explains:] "Here the debater is defeated due to non-employment of the probans."

[Dharmakīrti responds:] This is also irrelevant. Because there is no meaninglessness when simply it is proved that there is an utterance of a series of letters. If something is an utterance of a non-constituent of proof, only then it is meaningless. Because, the content of that utterance is not conducive to the proof of the probandum and also because it does not serve any purpose. Acceptance of it, (therefore,) as a special type (of the occasion of defeat) is not in order.

[A possible objection:] "It is no fault, because the word *vat* (= 'like') is used (in the definition)."

[Answer] It may be so. (You might say-) The term *vat* (= like) is used in the expression '*varṇa-kramanirdeśavat*' (= an act like uttering a series of letters). It indicates other discordant expressions also. Therefore there is no fault. But we do not accept this. Because, in that case no mention of 'Different point' etc. will have to be made (as distinct occasions of defeat). And in that case all those examples (of Different point) will have to be called the examples of Meaninglessness only, because they are covered by (the definition of the occasion of defeat called) 'Meaningless.'

[A possible objection:] "Meaningless utterance' does not mean the one which does not surve any purpose in proving the probandum. By 'Meaningless utterance' we mean the one which does not have any meaning."

[Answer] In that case, why is not any person, who is not a disputant at all (i.e. who does not participate in a debate at all), defeated when he makes meaningless utterances? Because, the efficient cause (= *nimitta*) is common (to the two cases).

[A possible objection:] "No. Such a case is not relevant in this context."

[Answer] Here you have to accept that the one who makes a meaningless utterance is defeated by that utterance only. This is common to all the persons who state a non-constituent of proof. All those who make meaningless utterances are worthy of being defeated by the same occasion of defeat.

Moreover, utterance of a series of letters is not always meaningless. In some context even that is meaningful. So this (= your mentioning series of letters as meaningless) is itself an occasion of (your) defeat, because it is meaningless here (= in this context). Moreover, you are saying something different (from what is relevant) when you say, 'Utterance of a series of letters is an occasion of defeat', because in that case one should mention striking the cheeks,[1] rubbing the upper garment[2] etc.

† § †

६३. [८.] "पर्षत्प्रतिवादिभ्यां त्रिरभिहितमप्यविज्ञातार्थम्।" [न्या. सू. ५.२.९] यद्वाक्यं पर्षदा प्रतिवादिना च त्रिरभिहितं न विज्ञायते क्लिष्टशब्दमप्रतीत - प्रयोगमतिद्रुतोच्चारितमित्येवमादिना कारणेन, तदविज्ञातार्थमसामर्थ्यसंवरणाय प्रयुक्तं निग्रहस्थानमिति।

नेदं निरर्थकाद् भिद्यते; सपदि प्रकृतार्थसम्बद्धं गमकमेव कुर्यात्, नास्यासामर्थ्यं, न च जाड्यात् पर्षदादयो न प्रतिपद्यन्ते इति न विद्वान्निग्रहमर्हति।

पर्षत्प्रतिभासपरिकल्प्यार्हवचनात् निग्रहार्ह एवेति चेत्। न्यायवादिनो जाड्यादुक्तमजानन् किं न प्रतिवादी निगृह्यते? जाड्यात् पर्षदादेः [२]अविज्ञातप्रतिपादनसामर्थ्य[२] इति विजेता न स्यान्न निग्रहार्हः। असम्बद्धाभिधाने निरर्थकमेवेति न पृथक् विवक्षितार्थं [विवक्षितम् अविज्ञातार्थं ?] नाम निग्रहस्थानमिति।

63. (8) [**Avijñātārtha:** Meaning -not- understood]

"'Meaning-not-understood' occurs when the statement uttered thrice (by the disputant) is not understood by the audience and by the opponent" (*NS* 5.2.9)

[**Vātsyāyana explains:**] "If the statement uttered thrice (by the disputant) is not understood by the audience and the opponent, because it contains obscure words or unfamiliar usages or is uttered too speedily or for some other reason, then such a statement the meaning of which is not understood and which is used for hiding one's capasity (to justify one's own position) is an occasion of defeat."

[**Dharmakīrti's response:**] This does not differ from 'Meaningless utterance'. If the disputant makes a statement speedily, which is intelligible and relevant to the topic under consideration, then he does not have incapability (to justify his position). Nor do the audience etc. fail to comprehend his statement because he was insensible. (But the audience fails to comprehend because of speady delivery.) Therefore such a learned disputant does not deserve to be called defeated.

[**A possible objection:**] "The disputant does deserve to be called defeated because the audience has only to imagine that his statement is capable.[1] (i.e. meaningful, *arha*)".

[**Answer**] Why is not the opponent (instead of the disputant) called defeated, who due to

२. (V): अविज्ञातप्रतिपादनासामर्थ्य - (R) and (D).

insensitivity does not understand the statement of the disputant arguing rationally? Or because his (= disputant's) capability to argue out the case is not understood by the audience and others due to their insensitivity, he (= disputant) is neither to be called the winner nor defeated. And in case the disputant is making irrelevant statements it is nothing but 'Meaningless utterance'. Therefore no separate occasion of defeat viz. 'Meaning-not-understood' may be proposed.

† § †

६४. [९.] "पौर्वापर्यायोगादप्रतिबद्धार्थमपार्थकम्।" [न्या.सू.५.२.१०] यत्रानेकस्य पदस्य वाक्यस्य वा पौर्वापर्येण योगो नास्तीत्यसम्बद्धार्थता गृह्यते, [३]तत्समुदायार्थापायाद्[३] अपार्थकं दशदाडिमादिवाक्यवत्। इदं किल पदानाम् असम्बद्धात् [असम्बन्धात्?] असम्बद्धवर्णात् निरर्थकात् पृथगुक्तम्।

नन्वेवमसम्बद्धवाक्यमपि पृथग् वाच्यम्; [४]नोभयसङ्ग्रहादपार्थकं युक्तम्[४]; निरर्थकस्य संग्रहप्रसङ्गात्।

एवंविधाच्च विशेषसमाश्रयात् पृथग् निग्रहस्थानलक्षणप्रलपनेऽतिप्रसङ्गोऽप्युक्तः। न च सङ्ग्रहनिर्देशे कञ्चिद्दोषं पश्यामः। प्रभेदे वा गुणान्तरमिति यत्किञ्चिदेतत्।

64. (9) [**Aparthaka:** Non-sensical]

"'Non-sensical' means an utterance which has no integrated sense, because earlier and later words in it have no connection." (*NS* 5.2.10).

---

३. In the light of *NBh* 5.2.10; तत्समुदयार्थोपायाद् - (R) and (D).

४. (V); नोभयसङ्ग्रहात् लक्षणमपार्थकम् - (R) and (D).

[Vātsyāyana explains:] "Where many words or sentences are known to be unrelated in meaning because there is no connection between earlier and later (words or santences), then it is 'Non-sensical' because it is bereft of integrated meaning, like the sentence beginning with 'Ten pomegranates'."[1]

[Dharmakīrti's response] This, they say[2], is mentioned separately from 'Meaningless utterance' which contains unconnected letters, because in this (= 'Non-sensical'), words (and not letters) are unconnected.

But in that case 'unconnected sentences' also will have to be mentioned separately. You cannot say that 'Non-sensical' as the occasion of defeat is legitimate because it covers both (unconnected words and sentences) because in that case (by the same token) 'Meaningless' would also be covered (by Non-sensical).

We have already said that it is a transgression (of reason) to prattle for defining separate occasions of defeat according to such peculiarities. We do not find any fault in referring to a collection (of cases by a single occasion of defeat). Nor do we find any special virtue in diversification. So this (Nyāya argument) is insignificant.

† § †

६५. [१०] "अवयवविपर्यासवचनमप्राप्तकालम्।" [न्या.सू. ५.२.११] प्रतिज्ञादीनां यथालक्षणमर्थवशात् क्रमः, तत्रावयवानां विपर्ययेणाभिधानं निग्रहस्थानम्।

न; एवमपि सिद्धेरिति चेत्। न; प्रयोगापेतशब्दतुल्यत्वात्। यथा- गौरित्यस्य पदस्यार्थे गोणीति प्रयुज्यमानं पदं ककुदादिमन्तमर्थं प्रतिपादयतीति न शब्दार्थाख्यानं व्यर्थम्। अनेन च पदेन गोशब्दमेव प्रतिपद्यते, गोशब्दात्

ककुदादिमन्तमर्थम्, तथा प्रतिज्ञाद्यवयवविपर्ययेणानुपूर्वीं प्रतिपद्यते, आनुपूर्व्या चार्थमिति। तथा हि पूर्वं कर्मोपादीयते 'मृत्पिण्डादिकं लोके, ततः करणम्' इति।

65. (10) [**Aprāptakāla** : Mistimed]

"'Mistimed' means utterance of the elements (of argument) in perverse order." (*NS* 5.2.11).

[**Vātsyāyana explains:**] "The elements of argument starting with Declaration follow an order due to their significance in accordance with their definitions. Hence stating the elements in perverse order is an occasion of defeat."

[**Udyotakara explains:**] "If one says, "No, because the proof (of the probandum) is possible in this way also", then we say, - No, because it (= an argument in perverse order) is like a word removed from the (standard) usage. For instance it is not correct to say that explication of the meanings of words is in vain because even the word '*goṇī*' used in the sense of '*go*' (= bullock) conveys an object possessing hump on shoulders etc. (i.e. a bullock). Here one apprehends the word '*go*' through this word (= *goṇī*) and then understands the object possessing hump on shoulders etc. In the same way one apprehends the elements of argument such as Declaration etc. arranged in their proper order through the elements which are presented in perverse order and then knows the meaning (of the argument) from the elements in proper order. That is why we find in this world that one first takes the object of action such as the lump of clay and then takes the instrument."[1]

† § †

---

१. In the light of V: ततः करणं मृत्पिण्डादिकं लोके - (R) and (D); ततः करणम्। मृत्पिण्डाद्युदाहरणमनेकधा लोके। NV, 5.2.11.

६६. तदेतदुन्मत्तकस्योन्मत्तकसंवर्णनमिव प्रयोगापेतशब्दवदेतदिति। यदि गोणीशब्दात् ककुदादिमत्यर्थे प्रतीतिशब्दान्वाख्यानप्रयत्नेन [? प्रतीतिः, शब्दान्वाख्यानप्रयत्ने न] अर्थं पश्यामः।

गोणीशब्दस्यार्थप्रतिपादनेऽसामर्थ्यात्। सत्यं दृष्टा, न तु साक्षादित्युक्तम्।

ननु गोणीशब्दादपि लोके प्रतीतिर्दृष्टा। सत्यं दृष्टा, न तु साक्षादित्युक्तम्।

उक्तमेतन्न पुनर्युक्तं; स्त्रीशूद्राणामुभयप्रतीतेरभावात्। यः खलु उभयं वेत्ति, शब्दमपशब्दं च, स एव प्रतिपद्यते। यस्तु नक्कशब्दं मुक्कशब्दमेव वा वेत्ति, न नासाशब्दं, स कथमपशब्दाच्छब्दं प्रतिपद्येत, ततोऽर्थं प्रतिपद्येत?

दृष्टा चानुभयवेदिनोऽपि प्रतीतिरिति।

न परम्परया प्रतीतिः; अर्थेऽसमर्थस्य शब्देऽपि प्रतीतिजननासामर्थ्याच्च।

न ह्यर्थेऽपि वाचकत्वं नामान्यदेव, अन्यत्र तद्विषयप्रतीतिजननात्।

अपशब्दश्चेच्छब्दे प्रतीतिं जनयेद्, अर्थ एव किं न जनयति? न ह्येतस्यार्थात् कश्चिद् भेदं पश्यामः, येन तं परिहरेत्।

अकृतसमयस्य शब्देऽप्यप्रतीतिजननाच्च।

न ह्ययमपशब्दः शब्देऽपि स्वभावतः प्रतीतिं जनयति, अदर्शनात् समय एव तु जनयेत्। समयवशात् प्रवर्तते।

एवं हि प्रतिपत्तिपरम्परापरिश्रमः परिहृतो भवति।

66. **[Dharmakīrti's response:]** Your saying that it is like a word removed from the (standard) usage, is like one mad person narrating another mad person's statement[1]! We do not see any point in (Grammarian's) attempt towards explication of (correct) words, if the apprehension of the object possessing hump in shoulders (i.e. a bullock) takes place from the word '*goṇī*'.

[A possible objection:] "The explication (of correct words) is made in order to explicate the meaning-conveying words, because the word '*goṇī*' does not have capasity to convey the meaning."

[Answer] But we find in the world that there is apprehension (of meaning) from the word '*goṇī*' also!

[Objection:] "True. We do find. But we have said that it (= the apprehension of meaning) is not direct."

[Answer] "You have said that, but what you said is not correct. Because women and *Śudras* do not have apprehension of both (= the correct word as well as the incorrect word).[2] Because only he will understand (the meaning from the incorrect word via the correct word) who knows both, the (correct) word and the incorrect word. But how will be the person who knows the word '*nakka*' or '*mukka*' but does not know the word '*nāsa*' (meaning nose) understand the correct word from the incorrect word and then understand the meaning? But we see in fact that the person not knowing both the words (but only the incorrect word) does apprehended (the meaning).

This apprehension does not take place through a series of relations. Because if a word does not have capasity to produce the apprehension of the meaning, then it cannot have the capasity to produce the apprehension of a word also.[3]

Because, 'the capasity to connote the meaning' (= *arthe vācakatvam*) (that subsists in a word) is not quite a different thing from 'capasity to produce the apprehension of it.'

And if the incorrect word does produce the apprehension of the correct word, then why does it not produce the apprehension of the meaning itself? We do not see any kind of dissension of it (= incorrect word) with the meaning due to which it would keep the meaning away.

Moreover the (incorrect) word cannot generate the apprehension of the correct word also, unless such a convention is made.

Because, the incorrect word does not produce the apprehension of the correct word naturally, because we do not see that. But it would produce (the apprehension) only if there is such a convention. The word operates on account of convention.

The exertion of (postulating) a series of apprehensions is avoided in this way.

† § †

६७. विपर्ययदर्शनाच्च। शब्दादर्थमप्रतिपद्यमाना अपशब्दैरेव ज्ञानं व्युत्पद्यमाना लोके दृश्यन्ते इति व्यर्थं शब्दानुशासनम्।

न व्यर्थं, संस्कृतशब्दव्युत्पत्त्यर्थमिति चेत्। कोऽयं शब्दानां संस्कारः? न ह्येषां प्रज्ञाबाहुश्रुत्यादिकं संस्कारं पश्यामः।

नाप्येषामेकान्तेन श्रव्यता। नाप्यर्थप्रत्यायने कश्चिदतिशयः।

न धर्मसाधनता, मिथ्यावृत्तिचोदनेभ्यः संस्कृतेभ्योऽप्यधर्मोत्पत्तेः।

अन्येभ्योऽपि विपर्ययेण धर्मोत्पत्तेः। शब्दस्य सुप्रयोगादेव स्वर्गमोदनघोषणा वचनमात्रम्। न चैवंविधानागमानाद्रियन्ते युक्तिज्ञाः।

न च दानादिधर्मसाधनचोदनाशून्यकेवलशब्दसुप्रयोगात् नगपातम् इति ब्रुवाणस्य कस्यचिन्मुखं वक्रीभवति। तस्मान्न 'संस्कृतो'[६] नाम कश्चिच्छब्दः।

---

६. (R); संस्कृतं - (D).

शिष्टप्रयोगः संस्कार इति चेत्। के शिष्टाः? ये विदितवेद्यादिगुणयुक्ताः। कः पुनरेषां गुणोत्कर्षानपेक्षोऽलीकनिर्बन्धो यत्तेऽमूनेव शब्दान् प्रयुञ्जते नापरान्? न चात्र कश्चिच्छब्दे ऽपरोक्षः[७] साक्षी, यत इदमेव प्रयुञ्जते नापरान् शिष्टा इति निश्चिनुमः।

नन्वेवं [न त्वेवं?] वयं गुणातिशयमपश्यन्तः संस्कारं केषाञ्चिच्छब्दानामनुमन्यामहे, तदन्वाख्यानं [तदन्वाख्याने?] यत्नं वा; गुणातिशयाभावात्। वेदरक्षादिकं चाप्रयोजनमेव 'अतत्समयस्थायिनः'[८]। सत्यपि गुणातिशये न करणीय एवान्वाख्याने यत्नः, तत्स्वभावस्यान्यतोऽपि सिद्धेः। प्राकृतापभ्रंशद्रमिडान्ध्रादिभाषावत्। न हि प्रतिदेशं भाषाणां किञ्चिल्लक्षणमस्ति। अथ च सम्प्रदायसाम्याल्लोकस्तथैव प्रतिपद्यते, तासां च प्रयोगभ्रंशं, तथा संस्कृतानां शब्दानां प्रतीतिर्भविष्यति। इति जडप्रतिपत्तिरेवैषा, या शब्दानां लक्षणे प्रवृत्तिः।

67. Moreover, (the incorrect words need not convey the meaning indirectly and correct words directly) because we find that converse is the case. Those who do not understand the meaning from the (correct) word are found acquiring knowledge from corrupt words. Hence the 'Instruction about words' (as given in Sanskrit Grammar) is fruitless.

[A possible objection:] "It is not fruitless, because it is meant for explication of Sanskrit (= cultured) words"

[Answer] What is 'being cultured' in the case of words? We do not see any (sign of) culturedness such as intellect or learnedness (in them).

Nor do these (Sanskrit) words have extreme audibility. Nor do they have any pre-eminence in conveying the meaning.

Nor are they the means to religious merit, because demerit is produced even from the

७. In the light of V; ऽपवाह्यः- (R) and (D).

८. (V); तत्स्थामवस्थापिनः - (R); तत्समयस्थायिनः - (D).

Sanskrit words motivating wrong attitudes. Conversely other words (= non-Sanskrit words) also produce merit. The grammarian's announcement that just the proper use of a word gives one the pleasure in Heaven, is merely an utterance. The experts of reasoning do not honour such (unfounded) scriptural statements.

Nor is it the case that one's mouth becomes tortuous if one says, "If there is only a proper use of the word, but it does not give motivation for acquiring merit through charity etc, then (instead of giving heavenly pleasure) it leads to collapse of a mountain."[1] Therefore there is no word which is cultured.

[A possible objection:] "Culturendness of a word means its having been used by learned persons."

[The counter-question:] Who are learned?

[Opponent's answer:] "Those who possess the qualities such as the knowledge of what one should know."

[Dharmakīrti's response:] What sort of a false conviction they (the 'learned persons') are having then, which does not require any excellence in their qualities? Because, they use only these (= Sanskrit) words and not others! Moreover, there is no direct witness to (the use of) these words, on the basis of whom we can ascertain that learned persons use only these words and not others.

We do not approve of culturedness of even a few words as we do not see any excess of qualities (in them). Protection of Vedas is a non-purpose according to the one who is not a follower of their system. And even if there is some excess of qualities (in the Sanskrit words), no effort needs to be made for their explication.[2] Because the particular nature of those words could be justified on some other basis also, like in the case of the words in *Prākṛta, Apabhraṁśa, Draviḍa, Āndhra* and other languages. There is no defining characteristic of languages belonging to the respective regions. People understand (meanings from words) in a definite way due to the sameness (i.e. continuity) of tradition, as they also understand deviation from the standard usage. The apprehension of Sanskrit words also will take place in the same way. Therefore tending to attribute defining characteristic[3] to words is an insensitive mode of understanding.

† § †

६८. अवयवविपर्ययेऽपि यदि तेषां वचनानां 'सम्बन्धप्रतीतिः'[१], न विपर्ययः नापि 'अर्थाप्रतीतिः'[१]; सामर्थ्यात्। न ह्यत्र कश्चित् समयः प्रत्यायनाविशेषेऽपि एवमेव '[२]अवयवाः'[२] प्रयोक्तव्या इति।

स एव तेषां क्रमो यथाऽवस्थितेभ्योऽर्थप्रतीतिर्भवति। इति न विपर्ययात् प्रतीतिः, तत आनुपूर्वीप्रतिपत्त्या प्रतीतिरिति चेत्। नाप्रतीयमानसम्बन्धेभ्यः आनुपूर्वीप्रतिपत्तिः।

येषां शब्दानां कश्चित् सम्बन्धो जायते [ज्ञायते?] 'इदमिह सम्बध्यते' इति, तेषु विदितसम्बन्धेषु कः कस्य पूर्वोऽपरो वा क्रमः, यो यथावस्थितानां सम्बन्धः प्रतीयते। न हि वाक्येषु पदानां क्रमनियमः कश्चित्, यथा राज्ञः पुरुषः, पुरुषो राज्ञ इति।

यावद्भिः पदैरर्थपरिसमाप्तिस्तदेकं वाक्यं, यथा-'देवदत्त गामानय कृष्णाम्' इति। अत्र पदानां यथाकामं प्रयोगेऽपि नार्थप्रतीतौ विशेष इति कश्चित् क्रमाभि-निवेशः।

---

१. In the light of V; सम्बन्धप्रतीतिर्न - (R) and (D).

१. (R); अर्थापत्तिः - (D) (No support from V).

२. (R); शब्दाः - (D) (No support from V)

प्रतिपादितं च प्रतिज्ञावचनान्तरेणापि यथा प्रतीतिर्भविष्यतीति। प्रतीयमानार्थस्य शब्दस्य प्रयोगेऽतिप्रसङ्गः। परिशिष्टेषु च सम्बन्धं प्रदर्श्य धर्मिणि भावः प्रदर्श्येत, धर्मिणि भावं प्रदर्श्य सम्बन्धः प्रदर्श्येत इति न नियमः कश्चिद्; उभयथाऽपि प्रतीत्युत्पत्तेः इत्युक्तम्। अप्रतीयमानसम्बन्धेषु च पदेषु न तेभ्य आनुपूर्व्या अपि प्रतीतेरिति नेदमपार्थकाद् भिद्यते इति नाप्राप्तकालं पृथग् वाच्यं स्यादिति।

68. (Now coming to the occasion of defeat proper:)

If in spite of the perverse order of the elements (of an argument) there is the apprehension of the mutal relationship[1] of the sentences (in the argument), there is neither false apprehension nor non-apprehension, then it is because the argument (with the elements in perverse order) has capasity (to convey the intended meaning).

Nor is there any convention such as 'the words (in the argument) should be used in this way alone' as there is no difference in conveyance (of meaning).

[A possible objection:] "That is the proper order of elements through which the apprehension of the meaning takes place. Hence there is no apprehension through the elements in perverse order. The apprehension of meaning through them takes place via the apprehension of proper sequential order."

[Answer] The proper sequential order is not apprehended unless the relation amongst the elements is apprehended. And if the relation amongst the words is apprehended as 'This is related here', then what would be their order of priority or posteriority on account of which they would be arranged? Because when the relation is apprehended, that itself is their order, viz. the relationship which is apprehended amongst them as they are. There is no rule governing the order of words belonging to sentences. For example '*puruṣo rājñaḥ*' (= Man of the king) and '*rājñaḥ puruṣaḥ*' (= king's man) (both are grammatically correct).[2]

Those many words constitute a sentence through which there is accomplishment of meaning. For example "*Devadatta, gām ānaya kṛṣṇām*' (= Devadatta, bring the black cow.) (The order of words = Devadatta, cow, bring, black.)[3] Here there is no difference in the apprehension of meaning although the words are used freely. Hence the adherence to order (of the elements of argument) is insignificant (*kaścit*).

Moreover we have explained how there can be apprehension (of the probandum) even without the statement of Declaration. If an implied word (or sentence) has to be used (explicity), then it would be a transgression (of reason). We have said with regard to the remaining elements that there is no rule that one should first indicate the relation (of pervasion) and then the existence (of probans) in the property-bearer, or that one should first indicate the existence in the properly-bearer and then the relation of pervasion. Because, the knowledge of the probandum arises in both the cases.[4]

If (on the other hand) (the order of the words in the argument is so perverse that) no relation is apprehended amongst the words, then the proper sequential order (amongst the elements of the argument) also will not be apprehended. Hence this case will not differ from the (occasion of defeat called) 'Non sensical'. In that case it will not be proper to mention 'Mistimed' as a distinct occasion of defeat.

६९. [११.] ''हीनमन्यतमेनाप्यवयवेन न्यूनम्।'' [न्या. सू. ५. २.१२.]यस्मिन् वाक्ये प्रतिज्ञादीनामन्यतमोऽवयवो न भवति, तद्वाक्यं हीनं; साधनाभावे साध्यासिद्धेः।

न [१]प्रतिज्ञान्यूनं[१] हीनं; तदभावे प्रतीतिभावादिति प्रतिपादितम्।

हीनमेव तत्; न्यूनतायामपि निग्रहादित्यपरः।

यः प्रतीयमानार्थमनर्थकं शब्दं प्रयुङ्क्ते, स निग्रहमर्हेत्, नार्थोपसंहितस्याभिधातेति असमीक्षिताभिधानमेतत्। अत एव प्रतिज्ञाया न साधनाङ्गभाव इति।

69. (11) [**Nyūna** : Insufficient]

"'Insufficient' means that (inferential statement) which is destitute of one of the elements." (*NS* 5.2.12.)

[Vātsyāyana explains:] "The (inferential) statement in which one of the elements, such as Declaration, is lacking, is deficient. Because the probandum is not proved in the absence of (complete) proof."

[Dharmakīrti's response:] If it is destitute of, say, Declaration, then it is not deficient, because we have explained that the knowledge of probandum takes place even in its absence.

Another one[1] says, "it is deficient, because even in the case of insufficiency (due to the absence of Declaration), defeat takes place."

This is an unthoughtful statement, because he will deserve defeat, who uses a redundant sentence (lit. meaningless sentence) the meaning of which is implied (by other elements of the argument), but the one who utters a meaningful (non-redundant) sentences is not defeated.

---

१. (R); Supported by प्रतिज्ञाग्रहणमुपलक्षणार्थम् - V; But the reading mentioned in V - प्रतिज्ञादीनां, and also (D).

Declaration is not a constituent of proof for the same reason.

† § †

७०. [१२.] "हेतूदाहरणाधिकमधिकम्।" [न्या.सू.५.२.१३.] एकेन कृतकत्वाद् "इतरस्य"[१] आनर्थक्यमिति तदेतन्नियमाभ्युपगमे वेदितव्यम्। यत्रैकसाधनवाक्यप्रयोगपूर्वको विचारस्तत्राधिकाभिधानमनर्थकमिति निग्रह-स्थानम्।

प्रपञ्चकथायां तु न कश्चिदोष:, नियमाभावादिति।

70. (12) [**Adhika:** Additional]

"'Additional' means that (inferential statement) which contains an additional probans or instance." (*NS* 5.2.13).

[Vātsyāyana explains:] "When the inferential statement is complete with one (probans or instance) the other one is redundant (Lit. meaningless). This is to be understood (as an occasion of defeat) when such a rule is accepted (in the debate)."

[Dharmakīrti's response:] When the discussion is based on (the rule of) using an inferential statement containing (only) one probans, stating an additional probans in such a discussion is redundant. Hence it is an occasion of defeat (there).

In a diffuse discussion there is no fault (of this kind) because there are no rules in it.

† § †

---

१. In the light of *NBh* 5.2.13. The word used in *NBh* is अन्यतरस्य; But इत्यस्य - (R) and (D).

७१. [१३.] ''शब्दार्थयो: पुनर्वचनं पुनरुक्तमन्यत्रानुवादात्।'' [न्या. सू. ५. २.१४] शब्दपुनरुक्तम्- अनित्य: शब्दोऽनित्य: शब्द इति। अर्थपुनरुक्तम्- अनित्य: शब्दो निरोधधर्मको ध्वान इति।

अत्र न शब्दपुनरुक्तं पृथग्वाच्यम्; अर्थपुनरुक्तवचनेनैव गतत्वात्। न ह्यर्थभेदे शब्दसाम्येऽपि कश्चिद् दोष:। यथा-

हसति हसति स्वामिन्युच्चै रुदत्यभिरोदिति।

कृतिपरिकरं स्वेदोऽङ्गारं [स्वेदोद्गारं?] पूर्धावति [प्रधावति?] धावति॥

गुणसमुदितं दोषापेतं प्रणिन्दति निन्दति।

धनलवपरिक्रीतं यन्त्रं प्रनृत्यति नृत्यति॥

यथा वा- यद्यस्मिन् सति भवति भवति, न भवति न भवति तत्तस्य कार्यमितरत् कारणमिति।

71. (13) [**Punarukta :** Repetition]

"'Repetition' means iteration (made in the course of argument) of words or meaning except as a confirmatory repetition."[1] *(NS* 5.2.14)

[Udyotakara explains:] "An example of Repetition of words - "Sound is impermanent, sound is impermanent." An example of the Repetition of meaning - "Sound is impermanent, sonority is subject to destruction."

[Dharmakīrti's response:] Here 'Repetition' of words need not be mentioned separately. Because it is covered by the mention of 'Repetition of meaning'. Because, there is no fault if the meaning is different even if the words are the same. For instance -

"The machine bought for a bit of money[2] is such that it laughts when the master laughs, cries loudly when cries, runs with a fastened Waist-band and with sweat coming out when runs, censures a virtuous faultless person when (the master) censures (the same), dances when dances."[3]

Or (another example) - "That which happens when this real thing happens and does not happen when it does not happen, is the effect of this, and the other thing is the cause.[4]

† § †

७२. गम्यमानार्थं पुनर्वचनमपि पुनरुक्तम्; नियतप्रदप्रयोगे साधनवाक्ये यथा प्रतिज्ञावचनमिति अर्थपुनरुक्तेनैव गतार्थत्वान्न पृथग्वाच्यम्।

अयमपि नियतसाधनवाक्ये एव दोषो वक्तव्यः, न विस्तरकथायाम्। व्याचक्षाणो हि कदाचिदसम्यक्श्रवणप्रतिपत्तिशङ्कया साक्षिप्रभृतीनां पुनः पुनर्ब्रूयादिति न तत्र किञ्चिच्छलम्।

नाविषयत्वादिति चेत्; नायं गुरुर्न शिष्य इति न यत्नतः प्रतिपादनीयः, येन पुनः पुनरुच्यते, इति पुनर्वचने निग्रह एवेति चेत् । न; साक्षिणां यत्नेन प्रतिपाद्यत्वात्, तदप्रतिपादने दोषाभिधानात्, प्रतिपाद्यस्य शिष्यत्वात्, विजिगीषु-वादप्रतिषेधत्वात्, त्रिरभिधानवचनात्, पुनर्वचनप्रसङ्गे समयनियमाभावाच्च।

72. **[Another type of Punarukta as stated in NS :]**

"That utterance is also called Repetition which expresses the meaning again which is implied (by other utterances)"[1]

[Dharmakīrti's response:] This (type of Repetition) occurs when the use of words in an inferential statement is rule bound. Utterance of Declaration is an example of this. This (type of Repetition) need not be mentioned separately because it is covered by Repetition of meaning.

Moreover this should be called a fault in that debate where the inferential statements are rule-bound, not in a diffused discussion. Because, (in a diffused discussion) the speaker sometimes says the same thing again and again by raising the doubt that witnesses and others have not heard (the statement) properly or understood properly. Hence there is no deception (of the opponent or the audience) here.

[A possible objection:] "No (it is an occasion of defeat), because this (kind of debate) is not the proper place (for repetitive statements). Here (i.e. in diffuse debate) the debater is neither a teacher nor a student; so he need not be addressed with efforts (i.e. elaborately) on account of which the same thing would be uttered again and again. Hence the repetition does amount to defeat."[2]

[Answer] That is not so, because (in such a diffuse discussion) the witnesses are to be addressed with efferts, because if they are not addressed with efforts then this is regarded as a fault; (secondly) because here the person to whom the explanation is addressed is a student (in a broad sense, i.e., someone worthy of being taught); (thirdly,) because (in a disffused discussion) the debate intended merely to gain victory is prohibitted; (fourthly) because 'making the statement thrice' has been mentioned (by you); (fifthly) because (in a diffused discussion) there is no conventional rule regarding repetition of an utterance.

† § †

७३. न चेदमधिकाद् भिद्यते इति न पृथग्वाच्यम्। विनियतप्रदप्रयोगे हि साधनवाक्ये आधिक्यदोष इति पुनर्वचनेऽपि गतार्थस्याधिक्यमेव पदस्येति।

प्रपञ्चकथायाम् [५]अनिरूपितै[५] कार्थसाधनाधिकरणायां नानार्थसाधनेप्सायां नानासाधनेप्सायां[६] वा श्रोतुः [७]हेत्वादि[७] बाहुल्यस्य पुनर्वचनस्य दोषत्वात्। प्रतीतप्रत्ययाभावाद् हेत्वादिबाहुल्यं वचनबाहुल्यं च साधनदोष इति।

---

५. (V); अपि कथितै - (R) and (D).

६. (V); नानासाधनेप्सां - (R) and (D).

७. (V); हेतुत्वादि - (R) and (D).

आधिक्यपुनर्वचनयोस्तुल्यदोष इति संग्रहवचनं न्याय्यम्; दोषाभावादेव गुणाभावात्, एवम्प्रकाराणां भेदानां वचने चातिप्रसङ्गादित्युक्तम्।

पर्यायशब्दकल्पो ह्यपरो हेतुः प्रतिपादिते विषये प्रवर्तमानः; प्रतिपाद्यस्य विशेषाभावात्।

अर्थः पुनः प्रतिपादनान्न भिद्यते।

73. Moreover this (= Repetition) does not differ from 'Additional', hence it should not be mentioned separately. Because, the fault of Additionality can occur in an inferential statement where the use of words is rule-bound. So in the case of Repetition also the word, meaning of which is already expressed (by other words) is Addition.

Plurality of probans' and Repeated utterance is not a fault[1] in a diffuse discussion. The diffuse discussion is such that it is not specified in it that the proof of a single object is undertaken; but it is desired to prove various objects in it or it is desired by the audience that one employs various probans (for proving the same object). It is a fault (in the debate where the use of words is rule-bound. Because, in such a debate there is no (second) apprehension (i.e. it is not permitted to generate second apprehension) of what is apprehended. So plurality of probans etc. and plurality of expression (in such a debate) is a fault of proof.

The fault in 'Additional' and 'Repetition' is equal. Therefore it is proper to express them in union. Just as there is no fault (in making their union), there is no plus-point (in mentioning them distinctly). We have said that mentioning varieties of this kind (distinctly) amounts to transgression (of reason).[2]

('Additional' can be included in 'Repetition of words'.) Because, the second probans which applies to the object argued out (by the first probans) is just like a synonym (of the first probans). Because, the object of argument is not distinct (in both the cases).

The (Repetition of) meaning[3] does not differ from arguing again (with additional probans or instance).

† § †

७४. यत्पुनरुक्तम्-"अनुवादे त्वपुनरुक्तं; शब्दाभ्यासादर्थविशेषोपपत्तेः"। यथा "हेत्वपदेशात् प्रतिज्ञायाः पुनर्वचनं निगमनम्" [न्या. सू. १.१.३९] इति। प्रतिज्ञाया एवं [एव?] गम्यमानार्थाया वचनं पुनर्वचनं, किं पुनरस्याः पुनर्वचनम् 'इत्ययुक्तं'[८] निगमनम्।

74. What has been said (by the author of *NS*, may be considered now) - "In the case of confirmatory repetition (= *anuvāda*), it is not a Repetition (as such) because (there) some special purpose is served by repeating words." (*NS* 5.2.15)

[Vātsyāyana explains:] "For example conclusion (= *nigamana*) is (defined by the author of *NS* in *NS* 1.1.39 as) restating the Declaration on the basis of probans."

[Dharmakīrti's response:] Stating the Declaration the meaning of which is implied (by the premises) is itself a Repetition, what to say about the restatement of it! In this way (stating the) conclusion is inadequate.

† § †

७५. [१४.] "विज्ञातस्य पर्षदा त्रिरभिहितस्याप्रत्युच्चारणमननुभाषणम्।" [न्या. सू. ५. २.१७] विज्ञातवाक्यार्थस्य पर्षदा त्रिरभिहितस्य यदप्रत्युच्चारणं तदननुभाषणं नाम निग्रहस्थानमप्रत्युच्चारयन् किमाश्रयं 'परपक्षप्रतिषेधं'[९] कुर्यादिति।

---

८. (R); इत्युक्तं - (D).

९. (R); supported by V. परप्रतिषेधं - (D).

उत्तरेणावसानान्नेदं निग्रहस्थानमिति चेत्। स्यादेतत्। उत्तरेण गुणदोषवता मूढामूढत्वं गम्यते इति किमुच्चारितेन? अस्ति हि कश्चिद् उत्तरेण समर्थो न प्रत्युच्चारणेन, नासौ तावता निग्रहमर्हेदिति। न; उत्तरविषयापरिज्ञानात्। यद्ययं न प्रत्युच्चारयति, निर्विषयमुत्तरं प्रसज्येत। अथोत्तरं ब्रवीति, कथं नोच्चारयति? तदिदं व्याहतमुच्यते- 'नोच्चारयति, उत्तरं च ब्रवीति' इति। अप्रतिज्ञानाच्च। न चेदं न [? न चेदं] [१]प्रतिज्ञायते- पूर्वं सर्वमुच्चारयितव्यं पश्चादुत्तरमभिधातव्यमिति। अपितु यथाकथञ्चिदुत्तरं वाच्यम् उत्तरं चाश्रयाभावेऽयुक्तमिति युक्तमप्रत्युच्चारणं निग्रहस्थानमिति।

75. (14) [**Ananubhāṣaṇa** : Non-reproduction]

"'Non-reproduction' means inability to utter the statement (of the other debater), the meaning of which is understood by the assembly and which is uttered thrice (by the other debater)." (*NS* 5.2.17)

[**Vātsyāyana explains:**] "The non-re-utterance of the statement, the meaning of which is understood by the assembly and which is uttered thrice (by the other debater) is the occasion of defeat called Non-reproduction, because if a debater does not (= cannot) re-utter (the other debater's statement), on what basis will be repudiate the opponent's position?"

[**Udyotakara explains:**] "If one says- "This is not an occasion of defeat because a debate is concluded by an answer (and not by the re-utterance)!", then we say: One may say so - "Whether one (= the respondent) is confused or not is known from the answer; what is the significance of uttering (the disputant's statement) then? Because some persons are capable of answering but not of re-utterance. He (= the respondent) need not deserve defeat just for that." If one says this then we say: No. Because, (inability to reproduce implies) the absence of comprehension of the

---

१. In the light of *NV* 5.2.17.

subject of answer. If he does not reutter, then the answer will be implied to be without subject. If he gives an answer, why does he not utter (the subject of answer)? So you are saying this contradictory thing - 'Does not utter (the statement) but answers it.' (One might say) "This is not so (i.e. Non-reproduction is not an occasion of defeat) because there is no declaration (to that effect). It is not declared (in the debate) that a debater should first utter everything (uttered by the other debater) and the answer should be stated afterwards." (we say:) The answer should be stated somehow. But answer without basis is improper. Therefore it is proper to regard 'not re-uttering' as an occasion of defeat."

† § †

७६. यदि नाम वादी स्वसाधनार्थविवरणव्याजेन प्रसङ्गादपरं घोषयेद्, विवादास्पदं च जिज्ञासितमर्थमात्रमुक्त्वा प्रतिज्ञादिष्वर्थविशेषपरम्परया अपरानर्थानुपक्षिप्य कथां विस्तारयेत्, तच्च सर्वं यदा नानुवक्तुं शक्नुयात्, कस्तस्य विवादाश्रयार्थमात्रोत्तरवचने सामर्थ्यविघातः, येन वादिवचनानुभाषणं निग्रहस्थानमुच्यते। तस्मान्न सर्वां वादिकथामननुभाषमाणो नोत्तरे समर्थः।

यद्वचनान्तरीयका जिज्ञासितार्थसिद्धिः, यथा पक्षधर्मताव्याप्तिप्रसाधनमात्रं, न तत्रापि प्रसङ्गान्तरोपक्षेपः, तदवश्यं साधनाङ्गविषयत्वाद् 'दूषणस्य'[२] उपदर्श्यत एव। तत्रापि न सर्वं प्रागनुक्रमेणोच्चारयितव्यं, पश्चाद् दूषणं वाच्यं; द्विरुच्चारणप्रसङ्गात्। दूषणविषयोपदर्शनार्थेऽनुभाषणे वादिवचनानुक्रमघोषणं व्यर्थमिति न कार्यमेव दूषयता। 'अस्यायं दोषः' इति नान्तरीयत्वात् प्रतिदोषवचनं विषयोपदर्शनं क्रियते एव।

76. **[Dharmakīrti's response:]** Suppose that the disputant incidentally announces same other topic under

२. (V); दूषणमेव - (R) and (D).

the pretext of explicating the object of one's own argument, states all the objects of inquiry on which there is dispute, in the course of Declaration etc. and then elaborates the discussion by introducing other topics in a special series of topics and suppose that the opponent cannot reproduce all that. Then what kind of failure in the opponent's capasity is there, in case he states only the answer to the subject on which there is dispute? Because, you call the Non-reproduction of disputant's statement an occasion of defeat! Therefore it is not the case that the one who does not reproduce the whole speach of the disputant is (necessarily) unable to give answer.

The statements with which the proof of the enquired object is invariably connected - such as that of existence (of probans) in the thesis-subject and the justification of pervasion - which are made without introducing some other topics in that, are (i.e. have to be) definitely indicated (by the opponent). Because, a constituent of argument is the object of refutation. But even there it is not obligatory to utter everything first in the same order and then to refute it. Because in that case there will be the undesirable occurrence of double utterance. If the opponent reproduces (the relevant statement of the disputant) in order to indicate the object of refutation, then announcement of the disputant's statements in the same order is of no use and hence should not be made by the opponent. Corresponding to each indication of fault, the object (having the fault) is mentioned, because there is an invariable relation of the form 'this has this fault'.

† § †

७७. न हि सर्वविषयोपदर्शनं कृत्वा युगपद् दोषः शक्यतेऽभिधातुम्; प्रत्यर्थं दोषभेदात्। तस्माद् यं पदार्थं दूषयति, स एव तद्दूषणविषयस्तदा प्रदर्शनीयः।

नापरस्तु; दूषणेऽपरोपदर्शनस्यासम्भवात्। तस्मिन् दूषिते पुनरन्योऽर्थोऽपरदोषविषय इत्ययमनुभाषणे दूषणे च न्यायः।

सकृत् सर्वानुभाषणेऽपि दोषवचनकाले पुनर्विषयः प्रदर्शनीय एव; अप्रदर्शिते दोषस्य वक्तुमशक्यत्वात्। तथा च द्विरनुभाषणं कृतं स्यात्। तत्र प्रथमं सर्वानुक्रमानुभाषणं निष्प्रयोजनम्। दूषणवादिना दूषणे वक्तव्ये [३]यन्न[३] तत्रोपयुज्यते तस्याभिधानमदोषोद्भावनम्। द्विरुक्तिश्च। इति सकृत् सर्वानुभाषणं पराजयाधिकरणं वाच्यम्।

तथाऽस्त्विति चेत्। स्यादेतत्। उक्तमेतदर्थान्तरं निग्रहस्थानमिति। तत्र साधने यतः कुतश्चित् प्रसङ्गादिना नान्तरीयकाभिधानं [ऽनान्तरीयकाभिधानं?][४] वादिनोऽर्थान्तरगमनमेवेति स निग्रहार्हः। न कश्चित् क्वचित् क्रियमाणप्रसङ्गो न [५]प्रयुज्यते[५], नापि तत् तस्यानुभाषणीयम्। न चेदमप्यस्माभिरनुज्ञायते- सर्वं प्राक् सकृद्वक्तव्यं, पश्चाद्दूषणमिति। किन्तु दूषयताऽवश्यं विषयो दर्शनीयः, अन्यथा दूषणावृत्तेरिति।

77. Moreover, it is not possible to indicate all the objects and then state the fault (in all of them) at once. Because, faults differ from object to object. Therefore the object of refutation which one is repudiating (at a particular time) should be indicated at that time, not any other. Because at the time of refuting one object indication of another object is impossible. After it is refuted, another object which is the object of another fault can be indicated. This is the proper way of reproduction and refutation.

If everything (that the disputant says) is reproduced at once, then the object (of refutation) will have to be indicated again at the time of stating faults in it, because a fault cannot be stated without indicating its object. This will amount to making reproduction twice. Out of them (= two

३. (R); यत्र - (V) and (D).

४. In view of the parallel discussion of अर्थान्तर in Sec. 61.

५. (V) and a parallel statement in sec. 33; प्रसज्यते - (R) and (D).

reproductions) the first reproduction of everything in the same order, is without any purpose; (on the contrary) when the opponent has to state the fault, stating something which is not pertinent to it, amounts to 'Not pointing out the fault' (= *Adoṣodhāvana*). It also amounts to duplication. Therefore reproducing everything at once should be called a ground of defeat.

[The opponent might say:] "Let it be so"

[Answer] You might say "We have said that 'Different point' is an occasion of defeat. While proving his own argument if the disputant states some point which is not invariably connected (with the main point) by bringing in some context or the other then it amounts to shifting to a Different point, and hence he deserves defeat for that. Nothing remains inapplicable if the context is created! However, such a statement of him (= disputant) is not to be reproduced. We are also not admitting that first everything is to be stated (by the opponent) once and then faults in that are to be stated. But (we admit on the contrary that) the object (of refutation) should be indicated by the opponent (in due time), otherwise the refutation will not stand!"

† § †

७८. एवं तर्हि नाननुभाषणं पृथग् निग्रहस्थानं वाच्यम्, अप्रतिभया गतत्वात्। उत्तरस्य ह्यप्रतिपत्तिरप्रतिभा [न्या. सू. ५. २.१८]। न चोत्तरविषयमप्रदर्शयन् उत्तरं प्रतिपत्तुं समर्थः। न ह्यनाक्षिप्तानुत्तरप्रतिपत्तिकमननुभाषणम्। तेनाननु-भाषणस्य व्यापिकायामप्रतिभायां विहितं निग्रहस्थानत्वम् अननुभाषणम् [अननुभाषणे?]। गव्यपरामृष्टतद्भेदायां विहितमिव सास्नादिमत्त्वं बाहुलेयेऽपि। तस्मादप्रतिभैव निग्रहाधिकरणत्वेन वा [वाच्या?] नाननुभाषणम्।

कश्चायं समयनियमस्त्रिरभिहितस्याननुभाषणमिति? यदि तावत् परप्रत्यायनार्था प्रवृत्तिः, किं त्रिरभिधीयेत? तथा तथा स ग्राहणीयो यथाऽस्य प्रतिपत्तिर्भवति। अथ परोपतापनार्था तदापि किं [६]त्रिरभिधीयते[६]? साक्षिणां कर्णे निवेद्य प्रतिवादी कष्टाप्रतीतद्रुतसंक्षिप्तादिभिरुपद्रोतव्यः, यथोत्तरप्रतिपत्तिविमूढस्तूष्णीम्भवति। न हि परोपतापनक्रमे कश्चिन्न्यायः, येन कष्टाप्रतीतप्रयोगद्रुतोच्चारिता निवार्यन्ते, त्रिरभिधानं वा विधीयते। न च परोपतापाय सन्तः प्रवर्तन्ते, शास्त्राणि वा प्रणीयन्ते इत्यदो वक्तव्यम्! तस्मात्तावद्वक्तव्यं, यावदनेन न गृहीतम्,। न [७]त्रिरेव[७]।

अग्रहणसामर्थ्ये प्रागेव वा परिच्छिन्नसामर्थ्येन परिहर्तव्यः [८]पुनरनुप्रतिबोध्येति[८]।

78. (On this we say:) In that case Non-reproduction should not be mentioned as a distinct occasion of defeat because it is covered by Non-imagination. Non-imagination means non-apprehension of the answer (to be given). The one who does not indicate the object of answer is not capable of apprehending the answer. It is not the case that Non-reproduction does not imply 'Non-apprehension of the answer'. Therefore since Non-imagination pervades (= covers) Non-reproduction, the occasion-of-defeat-hood that subsists in Non-imagination, subsists in Non-reproduction (too). For instance the property of possessing dewlaps etc. which subsists indiscriminately in all bullocks subsists (by implication) in *Bāhuleya* (= the bullock named as Bāhuleya) also. Therefore only Non-imagination should be called an occasion of defeat and not Non-reproduction.

Moreover, which conventional rule is this viz. "Non-reproduction of the statement stated thrice (is an occasion of defeat)"? If this practice (of uttering the statement thrice) is for the opponent's understanding of the statement, why should it be stated (exactly) thrice? He (=

---

६. (R) and (V); त्रिरभिधीयेत - (D).

७. (V); त्रिभिरेव (R) and (D).

८. (R); पुनरनुप्रतिबोध्य इति (D).

the opponent) should be communicated in such a way that he understands it. If (on the contrary) this practice is for troubling the opponent, then too why is the statement stated thrice? Instead of that he (= the disputant) should first tell the statement in the ears of the witnesses and then attack the opponent by making the statement cumbersome, incomprehensible, speedy and abridged so that opponent is confused in apprehending the answer and becomes silent. Because there is no rational rule regarding the way of troubling the opponent on account of which the cumbersome and incomprehensible expressions uttered speedily are prevented and thrice utterance is prescribed. It should be said here that good persons do not tend to trouble the opponents nor are sciences created for that. Therefore the disputant should speak until the opponent grasps, not necessarily three times.

If the opponent does not have capasity to understand then the disputant who has limited capasity should avoid him beforehand, by making (the witnesses) alert (to the fact that the opponent cannot apprehend the meaning of statements).

† § †

७९. [१५.] "अविज्ञातमज्ञानम्।" [न्या. सू. ५. २.१७] विज्ञातं पर्षदा प्रतिवादिना यदविज्ञातं तदज्ञानं नाम निग्रहस्थानम्। अर्थे खल्वविज्ञाते न तस्य प्रतिषेधं ब्रूयादिति।

एतदप्यननुभाषणवदत्रेति तत्रैव गम्यत्वादवाच्यम्। यथाऽननुभाषणेऽ-प्रदर्शितविषयत्वादुत्तरप्रतिपत्तिरशक्येति अनुत्तरप्रतिपत्त्यैव निग्रहस्थानत्वम्; उत्तरविषयप्रदर्शनप्रसङ्गमन्तरेणानुभाषणस्य वैयर्थ्यात्।

तथाऽज्ञानेऽप्युत्तराप्रतिपत्त्यैव निग्रहस्थानत्वम्। अजानानः कथमुत्तरम् उत्तरविषयं च ब्रूयात्? इति विषयाज्ञानमुत्तराज्ञानं च निग्रहस्थानम्। अन्यथा एवं सति अप्रतिभया [? अप्रतिभाया] निर्विषयत्वात्।

अनवधारितार्थो हि नानुभाषते, अननुभाषमाणो विषयमुपदर्श्योत्तरं प्रतिपत्तुं न शक्नुयादित्युत्तरं न प्रतिपद्येत; ज्ञातोत्तरतद्विषयस्योत्तराप्रतिपत्तेरसम्भवात्। उभयमेतदुत्तराप्रतिपत्तेः कारणमिति।

तदभावे प्रतिपत्तिर्भवत्येवेति तयोः पृथग्वचनेऽप्रतिभायाः को विषय इति वक्तव्यम्! निर्विषयत्वादवाच्यैव स्यात्।

79. (15) [**Ajñāna**: Non-understanding]

"'Non-understanding' occurs when (a statement made by the disputant is) not understood" (*NS* 5.2.17).

[**Vātsyāyana explains:**] "When a statement understood by the assembly is not understood by the opponent then it is an occasion of defeat called Non-understanding. Because if the meaning (of the argument) is not understood, he cannot make its repudiation."

[**Dharmakīrti's response:**] This (occasion of defeat) also is covered by it (i.e. by Non-imagination) and hence like Non-reproduction it should not be mentioned (separately).[1]

Just like Non-reproduction, it is an occasion of defeat via 'non-apprehension of answer' (i.e. Non-imagination), because there (i.e. in the case of Non-reproduction) the apprehension of answer is impossible since the object (of refutation) is not indicated; that is because reproduction will be of no use without the context of indicating the subject of answer; in the same way, in the case of Non-understanding also, it is an occasion of defeat, via non-apprehension of answer (i.e. Non-imagination).

Because, how can the one, who does not understand, speak out the answer and the subject of answer? Therefore not understanding the subject and not understanding the answer is the occasion of defeat. If that is not so (i.e. if they are not covered by Non-imagination) then in that case Non-imagination will be without any subject matter.[2]

Because, the one who has not understood the meaning does not reproduce; the one who does not (= cannot) reproduce will not be able to indicate the subject and apprehend the answer, and hence he will not apprehend the answer. Because the one who knows the answer and its subject cannot fail to apprehend the answer, as both these (= (1) Not understanding the subject (2) Not understanding the answer) constitute the cause of the non-apprehension of the answer.

The apprehension (of answer) does take place in the absence of these (= non-apprehension of subject and non-apprehension of answer). So you should tell me, what is the subject matter of Non-imagination, if these two (non-apprehensions) are mentioned separately (as the two kinds of Non-understanding)! Non-imagination (in that case) should not be mentioned at all, because it has no (distinct) subject-matter.

† § †

८०. नोत्तरज्ञानम् [? नोत्तराज्ञानम्]अज्ञानम्। किं तर्हि? विषयाज्ञानम्। ज्ञाते हि विषये उत्तराज्ञानात् तन्न प्रतिपद्येतेति अस्ति विषयोऽप्रतिभाया इति चेत्। एवं तर्हि अननुभाषणं निर्विषयम्; अज्ञानेनाक्षेपात्। न हि विषयं सम्यक् प्रतिपद्यमान: कश्चिन्नानुभाषेतेति नाननुभाषणं पृथग् वाच्यम्।

उत्तराज्ञानस्य चाक्षेपात्। विषयाज्ञानेनोत्तराज्ञानमप्याक्षिप्तमेव। न हि विषयमजानन्नुत्तरं जानातीति नैवाप्रतिभाया विषयोऽस्ति।

ज्ञातेऽपि विषये पुनरुत्तराज्ञानमप्रतिभाया विषय इति चेत्। एवं तर्हि विषयोत्तराज्ञानयोरपि प्रभेदात् निग्रहस्थानान्तरालवाच्यानि [निग्रहस्थानान्तराणि वाच्यानि?]। यथाऽज्ञानस्य विषयो ज्ञानम् [? विषयाज्ञानम्] उत्तराज्ञानमिति प्रभेदादसत्यपि गुणातिशये निग्रहस्थानान्तरव्यवस्था क्रियते, तथाऽज्ञानयोरपि सर्वोत्तराज्ञानमित्यादि प्रभेदान्निग्रहस्थानान्तराणि किं नोच्यन्ते? न चोभयस्याप्य-

ज्ञानस्य संग्रहवचने दोष:, गुणस्तु लाघवसंज्ञ: स्यादिति संग्रहवचनं न्याय्यम्। तस्मादननुभाषणाज्ञानयोरप्रतिभाविषयत्वान्न पृथग्वचनम्।

अपि च - न पूर्वोत्तरपक्षवादिनो हेत्वाभासाप्रतिभाभ्यामन्यत् निग्रहस्थानं न्याय्यमस्ति; तदुभयवचनेनैव सर्वमुक्तमिति। तदुभयाक्षिप्तेषु प्रभेदेषु गुणातिशयमन्तरेण वचनादरेऽतिप्रसङ्गात् व्यर्थ: प्रपञ्च इति।

80. **[Naiyāyikas may say:]** "Non-understanding does not mean not understanding the answer, but it means not understanding the subject-matter. Even when the subject-matter is understood, the answer may not be apprehended because it is not known. Hence Non-imagination has a (distinct) subject-matter."

[Answer] Then in that case Non-reproduction will be without subject-matter, because it is implied by Non-understanding. The one who apprehends the subject-matter correctly will not fail to reproduce it. Hence Non-reproduction should not be mentioned separately.

(Similarly Non-imagination too should not be mentioned separately.) Because, not understanding the answer is also implied. 'Not understanding the answer' is implied by 'not understanding the subject-matter.' The person who does not understand the subject-matter, does not understand the answer also. Therefore there is no (distinct) subject-matter of Non-imagination.

[Naiyāyikas may say:] The subject-matter of Non-imagination is 'not knowing the answer even if the subject-matter is known.'

[Answer] Then in that case, other[1] (intermediate?) occasion of defeat will have to be mentioned by classifying 'Non-understanding of subject-matter and answer' further. As you are accounting for a different occasion of defeat, by classifying Non-understanding into 'Not understanding subject-matter' and 'Not understanding the answer' even though there is no additional point (guṇātiśaya) (in doing so), in the same way (we ask,) why are other occasions of defeat not being mentioned by classifying 'Non-understanding' into 'Not understanding the whole answer'[2] etc.? Nor is there any fault in mentioning the two-fold Non-understanding unitedly; on the contrary there will be a plus-point namely 'economy' (lit. lightness). Therefore mentioning them unitedly is justified. Hence no separate mention of Non-reproduction and Non-understanding is justified because their subject-matter is the subject-matter of Non-imagination.

Moreover, any other occasions of the defeat of proposer or respondent, apart from Fallacies of probans and Non-imagination, are not justified, because everything becomes mentioned by mentioning the two. The elaborate classification is futile, because it is a transgression (of reason) to undertake to mention the subdivisions implied by the two (= Fallacies of probans and Non-imagination) (separately) without there being any additional point.

† § †

८१. [१६.] "उत्तरस्याप्रतिपत्तिरप्रतिभा।" [न्या. सू. ५.२.१८] परपक्ष-प्रतिषेधे उत्तरं यदा न प्रतिपद्यते, तदा निगृहीतो वक्तव्यः।

'साधनवचनानन्तरं'[१] प्रतिविषयमुत्तरे व्यर्थं तदज्ञानक्रमघोषणश्लोकपाठादिना कालं गमयन् कर्तव्याप्रतिपत्त्या निग्रहार्ह इति न्याय्यं निग्रहस्थानमिति।

81. (16) [**Apratibhā**: Non-imagination]

"'Non-imagination' means non-apprehension of answer," (*NS* 5.2.18)

[Vātsyāyana explains:] "When the other debater's position is to be repudiated by one, but the one does not apprehend the answer (to be given) to his (= other debater's) argument, the one is to be called defeated."

[Dharmakīrti's response:] After the argument has been stated (by the disputant) and when the topic-wise answer is to be given (by the respondent), if he (= the respondent) spends time in vain, by announcing (the disputant's statements) in the same order, reciting verses etc., out of ignorance about the answer, then he (= the respondent) deserves defeat because he does not know what he has to do. Therefore this occasion of defeat is justified.

† § †

८२. [१७.] "कार्यव्यासङ्गात् कथाविच्छेदो विक्षेपः।" [न्या. सू. ५.२.२०] यत्किञ्चित् कर्तव्यं व्यासज्य कथां विच्छिनत्ति। 'इदं मे करणीयं प्रहीयते, अस्मिन्नवसिते पश्चात् करिष्यामि। प्रतिश्यायकला मे कण्ठं क्षिणोति'– इत्येवमादिना कथां विच्छिनत्ति। स विक्षेपो नाम निग्रहस्थानमेकतरनिग्रहान्तायां कथायां स्वयमेव कथान्तं प्रतिपद्यते इति।

इदमपि यदि पूर्वपक्षवादी कुर्याद् व्याजोपक्षेपमात्रेण, न पुनर्भूतस्य तथाविधकथोपरोधिनः कार्यस्य भावे, तस्य स्वसाधनासामर्थ्यपरिच्छेदादेव विक्षेपः स्यात्। तथा चेदमर्थान्तरगमने एवान्तर्भवेत्; असमर्थसाधनाभिधानात्

१. (V); साधनवचनान्तरं (R) and (D).

हेत्वाभासेषु वा। प्रकृतसाधनासम्बद्धप्रतिपत्तेश्च निरर्थकापार्थकाभ्यां च न भिद्यते। अतिप्रसङ्गश्चैवम्प्रकाराणामसम्बद्धसाधनवाक्यप्रतिपत्तिभेदानां पृथग् निग्रहस्थान-व्यवस्थापने प्रोक्तः।

अथोत्तरवादी एवं विक्षिपेत्, तस्यापि 'साधनानन्तरम्' उत्तरे प्रतिपत्तव्ये तदप्रतिपत्त्या विक्षेपप्रतिपत्तिरप्रतिभायामर्थान्तरे वाऽन्तर्भवति।

82. (17) (**Vikṣepa:** Dispensation)

"'Dispensation' means breaking the discussion due to engagement with some work" (*NS* 5.2.20)

[Nyāya-explanation:][1] One breaks the discussion by referring to engagement with some duty or the other - "This work which ought to be done by me is getting lost; I will continue (lit. do) when that work is completed"; "The stroke of cold is damaging my throad." One breaks the discussion by the statement like this. This is the occasion of defeat called 'Dispensation'; one oneself brings the discussion to an end when the end of the discussion should be reached by the defeat of one of the two (debaters)."

[Dharmakīrti's response:] This too is an occasion of defeat if the proposer of the first position commits it only through a pretentious allusion, not if there exists a genuine (urgent) work which obstructs the discussion of that kind. There will be Dispensation (in the former case) because the lack of power of the disputant's own argument is identified. In that case this occasion will be included in shifting to a Different point. Or it will be included in the Fallacy of probans, because it is (a case of) stating an unsound (lit. incapable) reason. Moreover, it does not differ from (the occasions of defeat called) 'Meaningless' and 'Non-sensical' because it amounts to one's apprehension irrelevant to the proposed argument. And we have already stated the

१. (R); साधनान्तरम् (V) and (D).

trangression (of reason) involved in accounting for separate occasions of defeat corresponding to varieties of apprehensions irrelevant to the inferential statement (under consideration).

If on the other hand the respondent commits Dispensation, because he does not apprehend the answer, while he has to apprehend the answer immediately after the orgument (is made by the disputant), then that Dispensation (lit. apprehension of Dispensation) gets included under Non-imagination or Different point.

† § †

८३. ननु नावश्यं साधनदूषणाभ्यामेव सर्वस्य प्रतिपत्तिः, येन [२]सर्वा वादि-प्रतिवादिनोर्न सम्यक् प्रतिपत्तेर्हेत्वाभासेऽर्थे प्रतिभायां वान्तर्भावात्[२]। भवति हि अनिबद्धेनापि कथाप्रपञ्चेन विवाद इति। न; असम्भवात्। एकत्राधिकरणे विरुद्धाभ्युपगमयोर्विवादः स्यात्; अविरुद्धाभ्युपगमयोरनभ्युपगमयोर्वा [३]विरोधाभावात्[३]। तत्रावश्यमेकस्य वाग्वचनप्रवृत्तिः; युगपत्प्रवृत्तौ परस्परवचन-ग्रहणावधारणोत्तराणामसम्भवेन प्रवृत्तिवैफल्यात् स्वस्थात्मनामप्रवृत्तेः। तेन च स्वोपगमोपन्यासेऽवश्यं साधनं वक्तव्यं; अन्यथा परेषामप्रत्तिपत्तेः। अपरेण च तत्सम्बन्धि दूषणम्। उभयोरसम्यक्प्रतिपत्तौ हेत्वाभासाप्रतिभयोः प्रसङ्ग इति सर्वो न्यायप्रवृत्तः [४]पूर्वोत्तरपक्षोपन्यासो द्वयं[४] नातिपतति।

एतेनैव वितण्डा प्रत्युक्ता; अभ्युपगमाभावे विवादाभावात्।

83. **[The Opponent says:]** "But not everyone necessarily apprehends through proof and refutation, so that every improper apprehension, which either the disputant or the opponent has, is included either in Fallacies of probans or

---

२. I suggest सर्वस्या वादिप्रतिवादिनोरसम्यक्प्रतिपत्तेर्हेत्वाभासेऽर्थान्तरेऽप्रतिभायां वान्तर्भाव:

३. (R); विवादाभावात् (V) and (D). This reading seems equally tenable.

४. (V); पूर्वोत्तरपक्षोपन्यासोऽयं (R) and (D).

Different point or Non-imagination. Because debate is possible by way of unregulated diffuse discussion also (i.e. without mutual opposition or without any definite position)."

[Answer] No. Because that is impossible. There can be a debate between the two debaters holding contrary hypotheses on the same issue, because there is absence of opposition between the two persons holding non-contrary hypotheses or those holding no hypotheses. There (= in the debate between the two debaters holding contrary hypotheses), one of the debaters necessarily makes the first beginning of speech. Because any (two) persons with sound mind are not inclined to make the beginning at once because such a practice will be unsuccessful, because then understanding and grasping each other's statements and answering them will be impossible. The debater (with sound mind) should surely state the proof after presenting his own hypothesis. Otherwise others will not apprehend. The opponent too should state the fault connected with it (= proof). There will be the occurrence of Fallacies of probans and Non-imagination (respectively) if the two debaters (disputant and opponent respectively) have improper apprehension. Therefore any presentation of either first position or second (contrary) position, if it is based on logic, does not fall beyond (the jurisdiction of) the two faults (: the Fallacies of probans and Non-imagination).[1]

Negative debate (*vitaṇḍā*)[2] is ruled out by the same argument. Because there is no debate in the absence of hypotehsis.

८४. यदा तर्ह्यभ्युपगम्य वादं विफलतया न किञ्चिद् वक्ति, अन्यद्वा यत्किञ्चित् प्रलपति, तदा कथं हेत्वाभासान्तर्भावः?

असमर्थितसाधनाभिधाने एवमुक्तम्। अनभिधानान्याभिधानयोरपि पराजय एवेत्युक्तम्; अभ्युपगम्य वादमसाधनाङ्गवचनात्।

एतेनाधिकस्य पुनरुक्तस्य च प्रतिज्ञादेर्वचनस्य च निग्रहस्थानत्वं व्याख्यातम्। तदपि हि प्रतिपादितार्थविपर्ययत्वात्साधनसामर्थ्यविधानमप्रतीतप्रत्ययतया न लक्षणात् साधनस्य। असाधनाङ्गवचनमिति निग्रहस्थानमिति।

84. [**An objection:**] "But if a debater after stating the hypothesis in a debate does not say anything or chatters something different (i.e. irrelevant) because of frustration, how is this case included in Fallacies of probans?"[1]

[**Answer**] We have said so (i.e. that it will be included in Fallacies of probans) with reference to stating probans which is not justified. But we have also said that defeat (of the disputant) does occur in the cases of not stating (the proof). Because they are the cases of 'not stating a constituent of proof' (= *asādhanāṅgavacana*)[2] after stating the hypothesis in debate.

This explains in what way 'Additional', 'Repetition' and also[3] 'the statement of Declaration etc.' are occasions of defeat (lit. the occasion-of-defeat-hood of ....). That is because the power of argument is said to consist in not stating something which is already stated. That is because it produces an apprehension of what is not apprehended. It is not because the (Nyāya-) definition of argument is like that. It (= stating Declaration etc.) is an occasion of defeat because it is a statement of a non-constituent of proof (*asādhanāṅgavacana*).

८५. [१८.] ''स्वपक्षदोषाभ्युपगमात् परपक्षे दोषप्रसङ्गो मतानुज्ञा।'' [न्या. सू. ५. २. २१] यः परेण चोदितं दोषमनुद्धृत्य भवतोऽप्ययं दोष इति ब्रवीति, यथा-'भवांश्चौरः पुरुषत्वात्' इत्युक्ते स तं प्रति ब्रूयाद्-भवानपीति। स स्वपक्षे दोषाभ्युपगमात् परपक्षे तं दोषं प्रसञ्जयन् परमतमनुजानातीति मतानुज्ञा निग्रहस्थानमिति।

अत्रापि यदि पुरुषत्वाच्चौरो भवानपि स्यात्, न च [५]भवतात्मैवमिष्टः,[५] तस्मान्नायं चौर्यहेतुरिति यद्ययमभिप्रायः, तदा न कश्चिद्दोषः, अनभिमते तदात्मनि चौरत्वेन हेतुदर्शने दूषणात्।

प्रसङ्गमन्तरेणैवमृजुनैव क्रमेण किं न व्यभिचारित इति चेत्। यत्किञ्चिदेतत्। सन्ति ह्येवम्प्रकारा अपि व्यवहारा लोक इति।

अथ तदुपक्षेपमभ्युपगच्छति, एतदपि [६]उत्तराप्रतिपत्त्यैव[६] तत्साधने निग्रहार्हः। नापरत्र; स्वदोषोपक्षेपात्। तत्साधननिर्दोषतायां हि तदभ्युपगम एवोत्तराप्रतिपत्तिरिति तावतैव पूर्वमापन्ननिग्रहस्य परदोषोपक्षेपस्यानपेक्षणीयत्वादिति।

85. (18) [**Matānujñā** : Permitting (opponent's) view]

"'Permitting (opponent's) view' means implicating a fault in the opponent's position while accepting the fault in one's own position." (*NS* 5.2.11)[1]

[Nyāya-explanation:[2]] "The one who says, "This fault is committed by you too" without ruling out (one's own) fault indicated by his opponent, permits the opponent's view, because he implicates the fault in the opponent's position by accepting it in his own position. For example, when one (= the opponent) says, "You are a thief, because you are a man," the disputant would say to him "You too". This is an occasion of defeat called 'Permitting the (opponent's) view'."

---

५. (V); भवता नैवमिष्टः - (R) and (D).

६. (V); उत्तराप्रतिपत्तौ न - (R) and (D).

[Dharmakīrti's response:] In this example also, if the disputant means, "You too will be a thief, because you are a man. But you do not accept yourself to be so. Therefore this (= 'because a man') is not a sound probans", then there is no fault. Because it amount's to refutation of the disapproved presentation of probans (made by the opponent), by attributing thief-hood to his (= opponent's) self.

[A possible question by a Naiyāyika:] "Why is the variability of (probans-probandum-) relation not pointed out (= *na vyabhicāritaḥ*) in his (= opponent's) argument in a straight forward manner instead of accusing him (in a crooked way)?"

[Answer] This (question) is insignificant. Because such (crooked or indirect) linguistic practices are also (well-accepted) in people.

[Objection:]"But suppose he (= the disputant) is (actually) accepting his (= opponent's) infliction (and not pointing out the variability of relation) -"

[Answer] In that case too the disputant deserves defeat, because he does not apprehend the answer to be given to his (= opponent's) argument, not because he (= the disputant) inflicts his own fault upon the other debater. Because if his (= opponent's) argument is faultless, then accepting it is nothing but not apprehending an answer (to it). Therefore since the defeat has fallen upon him beforehand due to this reason only, 'inflicting a fault on the other debater' is not to be required (for declaring him defeated).

† § †

८६. [१९.] "निग्रहप्राप्तस्यानिग्रहः पर्यनुयोज्योपेक्षणम्।" [न्या.सू. ५. २. २२]पर्यनुयोज्यो नाम निग्रहोपपत्त्या चोदनीयः। तस्योपेक्षणं निग्रहप्राप्तौ सत्यननुयोगः। एतच्च 'कस्य पराजयः' इत्यनुयुक्तया पर्षदा वक्तव्यं, न खलु निग्रहप्राप्तः स्वकौपीनं विवृणुयादिति।

अत्रापि यदि साधनवादिनं निग्रहप्राप्तमुत्तरवादी न पर्यनुयुङ्क्ते, अप्रतिभैवास्योत्तराप्रतिपत्तेरिति न पर्यनुयोज्योपेक्षणं पृथग् निग्रहस्थानम्। न्यायचिन्तायां पुनर्न द्वयोरेकस्याप्यत्र जयपराजयौ; "साधनाभासेनार्थाप्रतिपादनात्,"[७] भूतदोषानभिधानाच्च।

86. (19) [**Paryanuyojyopekṣaṇa**: Neglecting the objectionable]

"'Neglecting the objectionable' means not claiming the defeat of the one (= the other debater), who has reached the defeat." (*NS* 5.2.22).

[**Vātsyāyana explains:**] "The word *paryanujojya* (= objectionable) means the one who should be objected by confirming his defeat. *Upekṣaṇa* of him (= Neglecting him) means not raising the objection when the defeat has been reached. This (occasion of defeat) should be spoken out (i.e. declared) by the council when it is asked, "Who is defeated.?" Because, the one who has reached defeat will not expose his own wrong."

[**Dharmakīrti's response:**] In this case also if the respondent does not object to the proposer of proof, who has reached defeat, then it is nothing but the case of Non-imagination, because there is non-apprehension of answer on his (= respondent's) part. Therefore 'Neglecting the objectionable' is not a separate occasion of defeat. If, however, the logic (of debate) is concerned, then there is neither victory nor defeat of either of the debaters here,

---

७. (V): साधनाभासेनाप्रतिपादनात् - (D): साधनाभासेनार्थाप्रतिभासनात् - (R).

because ((1) the proposer has not won because) due to the fallacy of proof there is no (proper) argument and because ((2) the proposer has not been defeated because) (his) real faults have not been pointed out (by the respondent).

† § †

८७. अथ कश्चिद्दोषमुद्भावयति, कश्चिन्न, न तदा निग्रहमर्हति; उत्तरप्रतिपत्तेः।

अर्हत्येव, सतो दोषस्यानुद्भावनादिति चेत्। न सन्त इति कृत्वा सर्वे दोषा अवश्यं वक्तव्याः।

अवचने वा निग्रहः; एकेनापि तत्साधनविघातादेकसाधनवचनवत्।

यथैकस्यार्थस्यानेकसाधनसद्भावेऽप्येकेनैव साधनेन [८]तत्सिद्धेर्न सर्वोपादानम्[८] इति न दोषमुद्भावयन्नेवापरस्यानुद्भावनान्निग्रहार्हः पूर्ववत्।

अथ पूर्वपक्षवादी उत्तरपक्षवादिनं निग्रहप्राप्तं न निगृह्णाति, तदा [९]तयोर्न्याये[९] नैकस्यापि पूर्ववत् जयपराजयौ; दोषाभासं ब्रुवाणमुत्तरवादिनं स्वसाधनादनुत्सारयतोऽसमर्थितसाधनत्वान्न जयो वादिनः; सर्वदोषासम्भवप्रदर्शनेन साधनाङ्गासमर्थनात्। नाप्युत्तरवादिनः; उभयदोषाप्रतिपादनात्।

तस्मादेवमपि न पर्यनुयोज्योपेक्षणं नाम पराजयाधिकरणमिति।

87. **[A possible objection:]** "Suppose the respondent discovers some fault but does not discover some other...."

[Answer] In that case he does not deserve defeat because he apprehends an answer.

[Objection:] "He does deserve defeat, because he fails to discover some real fault."

८. (V); तन्निष्ठेन सत्त्वोपादानम् - (R) and (D).

९. (R); तयोः - (D).

[Answer] It is not the case that all the faults must be spoken out just because they are real. Nor is one defeated just because there is non-statement (of some fault). Because even a single (real) fault vitiates the proof like the statement of a single probans.[1] That is as follows (= *yathā*). When there exist many probans for one (provable) object, all the probans are not employed since the object is proved by a single probans. Therefore the one who points out (only) one fault does not deserve defeat for not pointing out some other fault; as (we have argued) before.

Now if the proposer does not claim the defeat of the respondent who has reached the defeat, there is neither victory nor defeat of either of the debaters as in the earlier case. It is not the victory of the disputant (= proposer) who does not set aside the respondent from his argument when he (= the respondent) utters a fallacious refutation, because it amounts to non-justification of (one's own) argument on the part of the disputant. That is because he (= the disputant) does not justify the constituents of his argument by demonstrating the impossibility of all faults. Nor is it the victory of the respondent, because he does not point out any (genuine) fault.[2]

Therefore, Neglecting the objectionable is not a ground of defeat in this way also.

† § †

८८. [२०.] "अनिग्रहस्थाने निग्रहस्थानानुयोगो निरनुयोज्यानुयोगः।" [न्या. सू. ५.२.२३] निग्रहस्थानलक्षणस्य मिथ्याव्यवसायादनिग्रहस्थाने निगृहीतोऽसीति परं ब्रुवन् निरनुयोज्यानुयोगान्निगृहीतो वक्तव्यः।

अत्रापि यदि तत्साधनवादिनमभूतैस्तद्दोषैरुत्तरवाद्यभियुञ्जीत, सोऽस्थाने निर्दोषे निग्रहस्थानस्य नियोक्तोद्भावयिता न भवति तथा। भूतदोषोद्भावनलक्षणस्योत्तरस्याप्रतिपत्तेरितरेणोत्तराभासत्वे प्रतिपादितेऽप्रतिभयैव निगृहीत इति नेदमतो निग्रहस्थानान्तरम्।

अथोत्तरवादिनं साधनदोषमुद्भावयन्तमपरो दोषाभासवचनेनाभियुञ्जीत, तस्य तेन भूतदोषत्वे प्रतिपादिते साधनाभासवचनेनैव निगृहीत इति।

एवमपि नेदं हेत्वाभासेभ्यो भिद्यते। अवश्यं हि 'विषयान्तरप्राप्त्यर्थं'[1] हेत्वाभासा निग्रहस्थानत्वेन वक्तव्याः, तदुक्तावपरोक्तिरनर्थिकेति।

88. (20) [**Niranuyojānuyoga**: Objecting against the non-objectionable]

"'Objecting against the non-objectionable' means objecting to a non-occasion of defeat as an occasion of defeat" (*NS* 5.2.22)

[**Vātsyāyana explains:**] "The debater who because of his wrong understanding of the definition of occasion of defeat, says to the other debater, "You are defeated", even if it is not an occasion of (the latter's) defeat, should be called 'defeated', due to 'Objecting against the non-objectionable.'"

[**Dharmakīrti's response:**] Here too if the respondent charges the proposer of the argument, with the faults which are not there, then he does not become like that (i.e. defeated), though he attributes, that is, points out the occasion of defeat in the case of a non-occasion, that is, in a faultless argument. But he becomes defeated due to Non-imagination when the fallacious nature of his answer is brought out by the other debater, because he (= respondent) does not apprehend the answer, which is defined as 'pointing out a real fault'. Therefore it (=

---

१. (V); विषयान्तव्याप्त्यर्थं – (R); विषयान्तप्राप्त्यर्थं (D).

Objecting against the non-objectionable) is not a different occasion of defeat from that (= Non-imagination).

If on the other hand the other debater (= proposer) charges the respondent who points out some fault in the (proposer's) argument, with stating a pseudo-fault, then he (= the proposer) is defeated for stating a fallacious argument when the genuine character of the fault is brought out (by the respondent).

In this way also it does not differ from the fallacies of probans. One has to mention inevitably the fallacies of probans as an occasion of defeat in order to take other cases into account.[1] Once they are mentioned, mentioning the other types (such as 'Objecting against the non-objectionable') is redundant.

† § †

८९. [२१.] "सिद्धान्तमभ्युपेत्यानियमात् कथाप्रसङ्गोऽपसिद्धान्तः।" [न्या. सू.५.२.२४] कस्यचिदर्थस्य तथाभावं प्रतिज्ञाय प्रतिज्ञातार्थविपर्ययात् कथाप्रसङ्गं कुर्वतोऽपसिद्धान्तो विज्ञेयः। तथा 'न सतो विनाशः, नासदुत्पद्यते' इति सिद्धान्तमभ्युपेत्य पक्षमवस्थापयति - 'एकान्ता प्रकृतिः व्यक्तस्य[१]अव्यक्तलक्षणा; विकाराणाम्[१] अन्वयदर्शनात्। मृदन्वयानां शरावादीनां दृष्टमेकप्रकृतिकत्वम्। तथा चायं व्यक्तभेदः सुखदुःखमोहसमन्वितो गृह्यते, तत्सुखादिभिरेकप्रकृतिः' इति।

स एवमुक्तवान् पर्यनुयुज्यते - अथ प्रकृतिर्विकार इति कथं लक्षयितव्यम्? यस्यावस्थितस्य धर्मान्तरनिवृत्तौ धर्मान्तरं प्रवर्तते सा प्रकृतिः, यत् तद् धर्मान्तरं स विकार इति। सोऽयं प्रकृतार्थविपर्ययादनियमात् कथां प्रसञ्जयति। प्रतिज्ञातं चानेन - 'नासदाविर्भवति, न सत् तिरोभवति' इति।

---

१. (V); अव्यक्तविकाराणाम् - (R) and (D).

89. (21) [**Apasiddhānta:** Deviant thesis]

"'Deviant thesis' means first taking up a thesis (of one's own discipline for proof), and then making a point in debate without (following one's) discipline" (*NS* 5.2.24).

[Vātsyāyana explains:] "'Deviant thesis' may be known to be committed by one who after declaring some object as having such and such nature, makes a point in debate, going contrary to the declared thesis. For example a debater, accepting the thesis that "There is no destruction of the existent; nor does the non-existent came into existence" declares the thesis, "The original Nature (= *Prakṛti*) of the Manifest (objects) is one (Lit. single-ended). Because, the modifications of the Non-manifest are seen to be inter-connected with a single origin). For example it is seen that plates etc. made from mud have a single original nature (namely mud). In the same way the various manifestations are known to be inter-connected with pleasure, pain and delusion. Therefore they have the single (common) nature called 'pleasure etc.' (i.e. Prakṛti)."

He, having said this, is asked (by the opponent), "How should one define 'original nature' and 'modification'?"

(The disputant answers-) "When one (lit. another) property ceases and another property occurs, that which is constant (through-out this transformation) is the original nature. And the other thing (lit. property) (which ceases or occurs) is modification."

Here he (= the disputant) is making a point in debate by going contrary to the proposed thesis, without (following his own) discipline. Because, he has declared -

"The non-existent does not appear and the existent does not disappear."

† § †

९०. सदसतोश्च तिरोभावाविर्भावावन्तरेण न कस्यचित् प्रवृत्त्युपरमः, प्रवृत्तिर्वा – इत्येवं प्रत्यवस्थिते यदि स सत आत्महानमसतश्चात्मलाभमभ्युपैति, अपसिद्धान्तो भवति। अथ नाभ्युपैति, पक्षोऽस्य न सिध्यतीति।

इतोऽपि न कश्चिदनियमात् कथाप्रसङ्गो यत्तेनोपगतं 'नासदुत्पद्यते न सद्विनश्यति' इति तस्य समर्थनायेदमुक्तम् 'एकप्रकृतिकमिदं व्यक्तमन्वयदर्शनाद्' इति। तत्रैका प्रकृतिः सुखदुःखमोहास्तदविभक्तयोनिकम् इदं व्यक्तं, तदन्वयदर्शनात्। व्यक्तस्य तत्स्वभावताऽभेदोपलब्धेरिति।

सुखादीनामुत्पत्तिविनाशाभ्युपगमाभावात् सर्वस्य तदात्मकस्य नोत्पत्ति-विनाशाविति सिद्धं भवति।

90. When it is objected to (by the opponent) as - "There is no 'cessation of occurrence' of the existent except disappearance and there is no occurrence of the non-existent except appearance", at that time if he (= the Sāṅkhya disputant) accepts that the existent loses itself and the non-existent gains itself, then it is a case of Deviant thesis. If he does not accept, then his position is not proved."

[Dharmakīrti's response:] Here (i.e. in the above example) too there is no point being made in debate without (following one's own) discipline. For justifying what he (= the Sāṅkhya disputant) has submitted viz. 'Non-existent does not come into existent and existent is not destroyed', he says this viz. 'The original nature of the Manifest is one, because the inter-connection is seen.' (This can be explained as follows.) In this argument the single original nature means (the three strands-) pleasure, pain and delusion. The Manifest has its origin in these undivided (three stands). Because it (= the Manifest) is seen to be inter-connected with it (= the original Nature). The Manifest is of that nature because it (= the Manifest) is observed to be non-different (from the Nature). Hence it is proved: Because it is not accepted that pleasure etc. come into existence or that they are destroyed, everything which is of that nature, neither comes into existence nor is destroyed.

† § †

९१. अत्र तदुक्तस्य हेतोर्दोषमनुद्भाव्य विकारप्रकृतिलक्षणं पृच्छन् स्वयमयं [३]प्रकृतासम्बन्धेन[३] अनियमात् कथां प्रवर्तयति। तत्रेदं स्याद् वाच्यं - व्यक्तं नाम प्रवृत्तिनिवृत्तिधर्मकं, न तथा सुखादयः, व्यक्तस्य सुखाद्यन्वये सुखादिस्वभावता प्रवृत्तिनिवृत्तिधर्मतालक्षणमवहीयत इति। न तद्रहितसुखादिस्वभावता, व्यक्तलक्षणविरोधादिति, सुखाद्यन्वयदर्शनादित्यसिद्धो हेतुरिति।

एवं हि तस्य साधनदोषोद्भावनेन पक्षो दूषितो भवति। सोऽनुपसंहृत्य [४]साधनदोषं, कथां प्रतानयन्[४] स्वदोषं परत्रोपक्षिपति।

अयमेव दोषोऽनेन प्रकारेणोच्यते इति चेत्।

एष नैमित्तिकानां विषयः, न लोकः शब्दैरप्रतिपादितमर्थं प्रतिपत्तुं समर्थ इति, स एवायं भण्डालेख्यन्यायोऽत्रापि।

यथोक्तेन न्यायेन पूर्वकस्यासाधनाङ्गस्यासिद्धस्य [५]हेतोरभिधानादेव[५] निग्रहः, नापि नियमात् [अनियमात्?] कथाप्रसङ्गात् इति। इदमपि हेत्वाभासेष्वन्तर्भावात् न पृथग्वाच्यम्।

91. In this debate, he (= the Naiyāyika) himself who, not pointing out a fault in the probans stated by him (= the Sāṅkhya disputant), asks for the definitions of modifications and original nature, continues the debate without relation with the proposed topic and without following the discipline.

---

३. (V); पृकता सत्त्वेन - (R); प्रष्टा सत्त्वेन - (D).

४. (V); साधनदोषकथां प्रतारयन् - (R) and (D).

५. (R); हेतोरविधानादेव - (D).

Here it may be objected: "'Manifest' means that which is subject to occurrence and cessation. Pleasure etc. are not like that. If the Manifest is interconnected with pleasure etc., then it has the same nature as the pleasure etc. Hence its definition as something subject to occurrence and cessation becomes vitiated. Now the nature (of the Manifest) cannot be the same as that of pleasure etc. which are bereft of that property (viz. that of being subject to occurrence and cessation) because then the definition of the Manifest becomes contradicated. Therefore the probans viz. 'because the Manifest is seen to be interconnected with pleasure etc.' is unproved.

In this way his (= Sāṅkhya disputant's) thesis is refuted by pointing out a fault in his argument."

[Answer] Here he (= the Naiyāyika opponent) instead of demonstrating the story of the fault in the argument (directly), deceivers (the disputant)[1] and projects his own fault on the other debater (i.e. the disputant).

[A possible objection:] "The same fault (viz. Unprovedness) .is being stated (by the opponent) in this way."

[Answer] This is the province of the prophetic persons (lit. astrologers); (because, common) people are not capable of apprehending the meaning which is not expressed by words. The same allegorical principle of 'the picture drawn by a buffoon' (which we referred to before)[2] applies here also.

Here the (disputant's) defeat takes place in the way stated (by us) because of the statement of a non-constitutent of proof viz. the Unproved probans, which is employed before, and not because a point is made in the debate without following discipline. Hence this (occasion of defeat) should not be mentioned separately because it is included in Fallacies of probans.

† § †

९२. [२२.] ''हेत्वाभासाश्च यथोक्ताः।'' [न्या.सू.५.२.२५] हेत्वाभासाश्च निग्रहस्थानानि। किं पुनर्लक्षणान्तरयोगाद् हेत्वाभासा निग्रहस्थानत्वमापद्यन्ते, यथा प्रमाणानि प्रमेयत्वम्? इत्यत आह यथोक्तहेत्वाभासलक्षणेनैव निग्रह-स्थानभाव इति।

अत्रापि यथोक्तत्वाच्चिन्त्यमेव - किं ते यथा लक्षितप्रभेदास्तथैव, आहोस्विदन्यथैवेति? तत्तु चिन्त्यमानमिहातिप्रसज्यते इति न प्रतन्यते। हेत्वाभासाश्च यथान्यायं निग्रहस्थानमिति, एतावन्मात्रमिष्टमिति।

92. (22) [**Hetvābhāsa** : Fallacies of probans]

"Fallacies of probans as expressed before (are the occasions of defeat)."

[Vātsyāyana explains:] "Fallacies of probans are the occasions of defeat. (Here the question may arise-) Do the fallacies of probans assume the title of occasions of defeat due to some other defining feature as means of knowledge assume the title 'objects of knowledge' (on account of some other feature and not by virture of their being means of knowledge)?[1] Hence (Akṣapāda) says - "The title 'occasion of defeat' is due to the same defining feature of Fallacies of probans as expressed before."

[Dharmakīrti's response] Here too it is a matter of concern because (they say:) "As expressed before." Are the fallacies of probans to be construed as occasions of defeat in the same way as they are classified (in *Nyāyasūtra*), or in some other way? The issue, if discussed here will take us too far and hence we do not stretch it.

This much is acceptable here - The fallacies of probans, in so far as they are reasonably so, are occasions of defeat.

† § †

९३. लोकेऽविद्यातिमिरपटलोल्लेखनस्तत्त्वदृष्टे -

र्वादन्याय: परहिततरतैरेष सद्भि: प्रणीत:।

तत्त्वालोकं तिमिरयति तं दुर्विदग्धो जनोऽयं,

तस्माद्यत्न: कृत इह मया तत्समुज्ज्वालनाय॥

वादन्यायो नाम प्रकरणं समाप्तम्।

[कृतिरियमाचार्यधर्मकीर्तिचरणानाम्]

93. This logic of debate, which tears the curtain of the darkness of ignorance covering the philosophical vision of people, has been constructed by good persons engaged with the well-being of others. But these (other) misguided intellectuals (= *durvidagdha*) are converting this light of philosophical vision into darkness. I have made this effort, therefore, to brighten it (= the light) (again).

The treatise called 'The Logic of Debate' is complete.

[This is the work of the honourable Ācārya Dharmakīrti].

† § †

Notes

[The notes are numbered according to the section number occurring first and then the note-number within the respective section of the Translation.]

(1.1) '*Nigraha*' literally means 'arrest', and *nigrahasthāna* the place of arresting or the point of arrest. In this context '*nigraha*' means defeat and '*nigrahasthāna*' means point of defeat or occasion of defeat.

(1.2). By 'improper methods' the author means the ways such as *chala, jāti* and improper points of defeat. (See. *V*).

(1.3) I have used the words *asādhanāṅgavacana* and *adoṣodbhāvana* in the translation without translating them because Dharmakīrti himself interprets these words in various ways. For example *asādhanāṅgavacana* means (i) Non-justification of a constituent of proof or (ii) Non-statement of a constituent of proof or (iii) Statement of what is redundant as a part of proof or (iv) Statement of what is a non-constituent of proof i.e. a fallacious constituent of proof or (v) statement of something irrelevant to what is sought to be proved. (i) and (ii) can be clubbed together as insufficient proof (iii), (iv) and (v) can be clubbed together as the three kinds of statements of non-constituents of proof.' *Adoṣodbhāvana* means (i) Not pointing out the fault of the disputant or (ii) Pointing out non-fault as fault.

(1.4) *Artha* literally means object or matter (to be conveyed) but in the context of inference it rather means a state of affairs or a proposition to be proved.

(1.5) According to Dharmakīrti, statement of the inferential sign (*liṅga*, probans) with its three characteristics (*rūpas*) constitutes the argument or proof (*sādhana*). The argument should be further justified (*samarthana*) by pointing out that the probans does possess the three characteristics. *Asādhanāṅgavacana* here means either *non-statement* of a constituent of proof or *non-justification* of a constituent of proof.

(3.1) A proof contains two statements according to Dharmakīrti (i) The statement of *pakṣadharmatā* (which states that the probans exists in the thesis-subject) and (ii) The statement of *vyāpti* (= pervasion, which states that whatever has probans, has probandum). Here Dharmakīrti is saying that whether one states *vyāpti* as the first premise and *pakṣadharmatā* as the second or the other way about is immaterial as to the establishment of the thesis.

(4.1) I have translated *pramāṇa* as 'evidence' or 'means to knowledge' depending upon the context.

(4.2) Śāntarkṣita explains - 'विपर्यये। साध्यस्य हेतोर्वर्तमानस्य सतः इति शेषः।' Meaning- In the absence = In the absence of *sādhya* (probandum) in spite of the existence of probans.

(4.3) Literally - The entity which has as its defining feature, 'the absence of the description that it has some capasity', is indescribable.

(5.1) The idea is this. Suppose, we want to justify the thesis, 'Sound is momentary' on the basis of the probans 'being real'. For that we have to justify the statement of *vyāpti* viz. 'Whatever is real is momentary'. For doing this we have to be sure about the evidence (*pramāṇa*) which falsifies the negation of *vyāpti*. The negation of *vyāpti* could be stated as 'something is real, yet not momentary'. We want to show the absence of such a 'non-momentary real object'. It does not suffice to say that non-momentary real object does not exist because we have not seen any such thing so far. Because every kind of non-apprehension does not prove non-existence. So we have to produce some additional proof which may be given as follows - The 'real' by definition has capasity to function. So we have to show the absence of a 'non-momentary thing having capasity to function'. Non-apprehension (*anupalabdhi*) of a pervading characteristic (*Vyāpaka*) can be an evidence for the absence of the pervaded characteristic (*Vyāpya*). 'Succession or lack of succession' is the pervading characteristic and 'capasity to function' is the pervaded characteristic. That is, there is the pervasion of the form, wherever there is capasity, there is either succession or lack of succession. So the non-apprehension of 'either succession or no succession' in a non-momentary thing proves the non-existence of 'capasity' in it and non-existence of capasity implies unreality.

(5.2) The infinite regress would occur if one *vyāpti* is proved on the basis of another and that on the basis of the third and so on and so forth.

(6.1) The opponent seems to argue that the non-apprehension would be useful according to you, because non-apprehension of the pervader would prove the non-existence of the pervaded. But this non-apprehension would not be useful if the pervasion itself is not proved.

(6.2) *Arvāk-darśana* may mean either someone having down-word vision or having proximate vision.

(7.1) While elaborating the point Dharmakīrti is repeating the point which he had made earlier. Śāntarakṣita, rightly points this out. But he gives an alternative interpretation of the passage in order to avoid the charge of repetition. He interprets this as response to the opponent's objection viz. "How is a probans not faulty if it is supported by a falsifying evidence." I am, however, not following Śāntarakṣita's interpretation here. As a matter of fact Dharmakīrti is repetitive in his elaboration of *svabhāvānumāna.*

(7.2) Here the word *mātra* cannot be taken to mean 'only.'. Because then 'साधनधर्ममात्रान्वयः साध्यधर्मस्य' would imply "Only that which has probans has probandum." But this is not pervasion proper but the converse of it. Śāntarakṣita is aware of this when he says - न त्वेवं करणीयं साधन-धर्ममात्रेणान्वयः साध्यधर्मेति। एवं हि साध्यमेव हेतुना अविनाभूतं जातं न हेतुरिति हेतोरगमकत्वं भवेत्। But *mātra* can be translated as 'all' or 'whole' as I have done.

(8.1) Śāntarakṣita explains: '*Samartheṣu tadhetuṣu*' refers to other causal conditions (but not 'the cause') For example air, fuel etc. are causal conditions of the smoke, but fire is the cause.

(8.2) The idea may be explained with reference to smoke-fire example as follows. For establishing negative concomitance between smoke and fire, it does not suffice to demonstrate that when fire (= the cause) is not there smoke (= the effect) is also not there. Because, one may doubt that smoke may not be there, because, say, fuel was not there. So one has to show that other conditions (such as fuel, air) being present, smoke is not there when fire is not there.

(9.1) '*upalabdhilakṣaṇaprāpta*' literally means that which has arrived at the condition of apprehension. By implication it means 'apprehensible', i.e. which fulfils the condition of apprehensibility.

(9.2) Śāntarakṣita interprets *pratipattuḥ* as *prativādinaḥ* (= of the opponent). He suggests that the object, the absence of which is proved by the disputant on the basis of non-apprehension should be apprehensible by the opponent.

That is, it does not suffice if it is apprehensible by the disputant himself but not apprehensible by the opponent. I have however translated '*pratipattṛ*' as 'knower'.

(9.3) The 'practice of non-existence' means either the linguistic practice in terms of non-existence or any practice which is concerned with non-existence of a certain object. It may also indicate the cognition of non-existence.

(9.4) The three fold remoteness of the object is (i) remoteness in space (ii) remoteness in time and (iii) remoteness by self-nature of the object. As Śāntarakṣita explains - त्रिविधेन विप्रकर्षेण व्यवधानेन देशकालस्वभावलक्षणेन ...।

(12.1) Dharmakīrti has said ".... Because, if the object of this kind exists and the other conditions of apprehension are present, then there will not be non-apprehension" (See Sec. 10) so the apprehension of the object which is possible because the object fulfils the conditions of apprehensibility and because other conditions are also present, gives rise to the practice of existence.

(13.1) These examples are given by Dharmakīrti to show that many a time cognition or description of an object may not match with the true nature of the object. Sometimes an object is described as real, but in fact it is unreal because it is no more. (For example, 'King Mahāsammata'). Sometimes the object is unreal because it is an event which is yet to happen (For example, 'Śaṅkha elevating sacrificial post'). Sometimes the object is a non-entity (e.g. the horn of a hare). Sometimes the object is one but it is described in too many words because it has multiple functions. (For instance colour which is perceptual and is restrictive because it prohibits the existence of other objects in its own location). Sometimes the object is in fact complex but it is described by a single term. (For example 'pot' which is a cluster (*saṅghāta*) of many objects is called by a single term because its function (to carry water etc.) is singular.)

(14.1) I have suggested 'अनेकसम्बन्धिनम्' in place of 'अनेकं सम्बन्धिनम्' in the light of *V.* 'अनेकसम्बन्धिन्' seems to refer to the relation of *samavāya* which relates itself with many relata. Especially in the case of *avayava-avayavi* - relation *samavāya* relates one composite object (*avayavin*) with all its parts (*avayavas*).

(14.2) An endless series (infinite regress) would occur, if *samavāya* is accepted for explaining one-many relation. Because, then *samavāya* (which is one) will have to be related with many relata, by another *samavāya* and so on ad infinitum.

(14.3) Vaiśeṣikas think that although pot is an outcome of a collection of many elements it is a different object from the collection of those elements. (It is *avayavin* and not mere *saṁghāta*). The pot is related with its elements by the relation called *samavāya.* If pot were not a different object, we would not have used a different word for it. Here Dharmakīrti argues that use of a different word does not imply the existence of a different entity. The same entity can assume different descriptions or nomenclatures in accordance with different functions. Similarly many things having a common collective function may assume a singular name.

(16.1) Vaiśeṣikas hold that substance (*dravya*) is the substratum of many qualities out of which *rūpa* (colour) could be one. If one and the same substance can be related as the substratum with many qualities, why cannot one and the same word, say, 'pot' be related as the name with many objects which are the constituents of the pot?

(16.2) There is a pun on the word 'असद्भूत' It means (1) false and also (2) the ghost of falsehood. The word अभिनिवेश (= involvement, adherence, being possessed) applies to both.

(16.3) Here the opponent intends to say that *rūpa* as *rūpa* may be common to many objects, although the function of *rūpa* in one object is different from that in another object. Here we still use the same word *rūpa* for different occurrences of *rūpa*, although every occurrence corresponds to a different pragmatic function.

(16.4) That is to say, if a particular colour is common to many objects of the same type, it will not have different (i.e. exclusive) function differing from object to object, but it will be one and the same in the case of all objects and consequently the colour occurring in various objects can be mentioned by a single word.

(16.5) The point is: We do have perceptual knowledge of distinct colour-apprearances in spite of the inclination of our opponents to claim that the colour is common to all collections having that colour.

(17.1) Literally: Cover, Shell.

(17.2) Dharmakīrti intends to say: If according to you (i.e. the Vaiśeṣika) the pot exists as a distinct entity apart from its constituents such as colour, then the pot should be perceptible independently of any colour. But we never perceive a pot bereft of all colours. So the Vaiśeṣika view that pot is distinct from its colour, must be false.

(17.3) Dharmakīrti is giving these examples for supporting his own argument that if pot exists distinctly apart from its constituents, then it should appear as distinct, bereft of its colour etc. Odour and taste of the same eatable are distinct although they are located in the same eatable, and they also appear distinctly. Similarly the touch of wind and the touch of sun's heat also appear distinctly and they are distinct, although they are objects of the same sense-organ. Similarly pot and its colour should appear independently of each other if they are distinct entities.

(17.4) 'अमूल्यदानक्रयी' —— A person who tries to purchase things without paying their price. Here 'pot' as conceived by Vaiśeṣikas is compared with such a person. Pot as conceived by Vaiśeṣikas tries to obtain distinct perceptible existence without paying its price, that is, without exhibiting its own distinct nature.

(18.1) This completes one unit of discussion which begins from section 13. The claim that was made in section 13, was that all cognitions, verbal usages or distinctions and identities among the same do not prove the *existence* of the corresponding objects or distinctions or identities among the objects (respectively). Dharmakīrti established the claim with special reference to the existence of pot as an entity distinct from its colour etc. He established that although a different word 'pot' is used for the collection of colour etc., it does not establish the distinctness of the entity called pot. He is here concluding the discussion by generalising the claim with reference to all cognitions, verbal usages etc.

(18.2) Here the Vaiśeṣikas seem to be arguing that in fact the composite object such as pot is perceptual (so there is no need to *infer* its existence), but we are providing arguments for its proof because sometimes it is not clearly perceived when its perception is dominated by some other object (say, colour). Dharmakīrti is saying that it is not proper to argue in this way. Because at least sometimes the perception of a composite object should not be dominated and when it is not dominated, the colour etc. should be identified as distinct from the composite object. But in fact it is never identified distinctly. So your attempt to provide inferences for proving composite object (= *Avayavī*) is not satisfactory.

(18.3) In section 12 Dharmakīrti referred to three reasons on the basis of which existence may be established - cognition, verbal usage and pragmatic function. Here he arrives at a conclusion with regard to cognition and verbal usage. He claims that they cannot always (unconditionally) establish the existence. In the next section he is considering the question with reference to pragmatic function.

(19.1) Here Dharmakīrti is claiming that although the collection of threads which is called cloth is different from the collection of threads which is simply called a collection of threads and not a cloth, because their causal conditions (*pratyayas*) are different, although both of them belong to the same series of modifications (*santati* of *saṁskāras*). The collection of threads which is called cloth is nothing over and above collection of threads. It has a different function, because it is a product of different causal conditions. The difference in function does not establish the distinct existence of a composite whole (*avayāvī*) over and above its parts.

(19.2) That is to say, according to Dharmakīrti, just as the sameness or distinctness of pragmatic functions cannot establish same or distinct existences of an object, similarly sameness or distinctness of cognition or appellation too does not establish sameness or distinctness of the existences. In fact Dharmakīrti has given an independent argument for the latter part of his position in sections 13 to 17.

(20.1) The earlier statement about non-apprehension was made in the section 9.

(20.2) Here Dharmakīrti is suggesting that just as non-existence of pot can be proved on the basis of its qualified non-apprehension (i.e. non-apprehension qualified by fulfillment of the condition of apprehensibility), similarly many other Vaiśeṣika *padārthas* such as composite objects (*avayavī*), universals (*sāmānya*), Inherence (*samavāya*) etc. could be proved to be non-existent on the basis of qualified non-apprehension.

(20.3) This concludes one major argument regarding the nature of non-apprehension as the reason for proving non-existence. This argument started from section 9. In this Dharmakīrti was mainly combating Vaiśeṣikas. In the next section he is starting his argument with Sāṅkhyas.

(21.1) This opponent is a Sāṅkhya philosopher according to Śāntarakṣita. This whole section (21) is devoted to the discussion of the objection of Sāṅkhyas according to which everything is existent either in manifest or non-manifest form, so that the question of non-apprehension as the reason for proving non-existence does not arise.

(21.2) The idea is this: According to the Sāṅkhya opponent the linguistic practice of non-existnece is untenable. But this position may cause disorder in his systematisation. The Sāṅkhya opponent wants to remove the disorder by taking recourse to "disappearance and appearance of the states of a thing". For instance he would say: The curd was not non-existent in the milk; only it was non-manifest. Now Dharkamīrti argues; Even the idea of 'Not being manifest' is untenable if the practice of 'Non-existence' is not accepted. Because, the distinction between manifest and non-manifest state is nothing but the distinction between existence and non-existence of manifestation.

(21.3) By 'positive evidence' (*vidhi*) Śāntarakṣita understands the varieties of contrary apprehensions such as '*Svabhāvaviruddhopalambha*' (For example: - "This thing cannot be wet with water because it is full of fire") and by 'negative evidence' (*pratiṣedha*) he understands the varieties of non-apprehensions such as *Vyāpakānupalabdhi* (For example - "Here there is no smoke because no fire is seen.")

(22.1) '*Vyabhicāra*' denotes a case where probans exists without probandum. Here 'Non-availability of inference' is the probans and 'the absence of the object' is the probandum. Here Dharmakīrti points out that sometimes an object may be present but no inference for proving it may be present. Hence there is *Vyabhicāra.*

(22.2) सर्वप्रत्यक्षनिवृत्ति: - (Lit-) the cessation of perceptions by all beings. Here Dharmakīrti is pointing out that that an object is not perceived by any being (*sarvapratyakṣanivṛthiḥ*) cannot be proved (*asiddha*). This is a response to the opponent's argument which may be expressed as follows, "The object is absent because *no one perceives it.*" Dharmakīrti claims that this probans cannot be proved.

(22.3) Here Dharmakīrti is stating the general rule regarding the knowledge of non-existence (rather, regarding the correct practice of non-existence). Suppose that there is a *pramāṇa* P which *necessarily* proves E (= existence an object of specific nature). The specific nature of the object is such that if the object exists then it must be known through P. If the object has this specific nature then the non-availability of P can lead to the knowledge of Non - E (Non-existence of the object). That is, if E implies availability of P then Non-availability of P implies Non-E.

(22.4) A Sāṅkhya philosopher, for instance, may claim that the curd which is latent in milk fulfils the condition of apprehensibility. Yet it is not perceived in the milk, but it is inferred to be there. So 'non-apprehension' should include non-availability of inference also. Dharmikīrti is denying this position because for him if curd *is* apprehensible, but not apprehended perceptually in the milk, then it is non-existent there.

(23.1) Śāntarakṣita interprets it as 'cessation of one excess and generation of another excess' and explains this Sāṅkhya argument as follows: When we say that milk has become curd now, we are saying that curd was in non-manifest state, now the non-manifest state has ceased to exist and the manifest state has come into existence. He seems to accept the reading 'नैकातिशयनिवृत्त्या' in place of 'नानतिशयनिवृत्त्या'; But he himself refers to the other reading also 'पर: प्राह नानतिशय: इति।' If we synthesize both the readings, we could possibly reconstruct it as follows 'नानतिशय:। एकातिशयनिवृत्त्या ...' The translation follows this reconstructed reading.

(23.2) I have translated '*anvaya*' as continuous capasity or continuity, This continuity is the continuous capasity to get destroyed and to be generated.

(23.3) We call something as milk (and not as curd) and something as curd (and not as milk). If there is continuity (*anvaya*) without any change, then there will be no significant distinction between the two practices.

(24.1) Two 'modalities' correspond with two view points from which a change can be described. 'State' is one modality and 'capasity' is another. States get generated and destroyed. They are many in number and are perceptible. But the capasity is continuous, without generation or destruction. It is one and imperceptible. So a thing is subject to generation etc.; it is many and perceptible from 'state' point of view. But it is continuous, one and imperceptible from 'capasity' point of view. This appears to be the Sāṅkhya view. The languages of '*paryāyas*' (modalities), however, suits more to the Jaina approach than to Sāṅkhya approach. (I have not followed Śāntarakṣita's interpretation, according to which, the oneness of state and capasity is one modality but their distinction is the absolute truth (परमार्थतस्तु भेद एव).

(24.2) According to Sāṅkhya system pleasure, pain and delusion (= *sukha, duḥkha* and *moha*) are the different strands that constitute *Prakṛti*. They are irreducible to each other. The difference between them can be established on the basis of their distinct cognitions or appearances. Similarly *Puruṣas* (conscious beings) are many and distinct from each other. Their difference can be established on the basis of our experience to the effect that cognitions and awareness that one person has are different from those another person has.

(24.3) Śāntarakṣita comments that according to Dharmakīrti *Śakti* (capasity, power) of a thing cannot *arise* from a thing because it is always present in the thing. Otherwise *śakti* will be indistinguishable from a 'state'. A state of a thing can be said to arise from a thing. *Śakti,* however is not identical with the thing which is the locus of *śakti.*

(25.1) According to Buddhists 'properties' and 'substances' are not distinct reals. Still one and the same thing can be said to have different properties relative to different points of view. (The different points of view correlate with the different kinds of things from which the given thing needs to be excluded or differentiated. For example when a pot is characterised as impermanent, the pot and its characteristic namely impermanence are not two distinct reals. The pot may also be characterised as black. Again 'the pot' and 'black' are not two distinct reals. Still 'impermanence' and 'blackness' do not mean the same thing. Because the pot is described as impermanent subject to the inquiry about the pot whether it is permanent or not, And it is described as black subject to the inquiry about its colour.

But this alternative view-point is not available to a Sāṅkhya philosopher.

(25.2) Sāṅkhyas say that the conscious substance (*Puruṣa*) does not undergo any transformation whereas *Prakṛti* does. But if cessation and arisal of one thing can amount to transformation of another thing then the former in *Prakṛti* can amount to the latter in *Puruṣa.*

(25.3) A Buddhist may approve of the linguistic usage 'Mud has been transformed into a pot'. But he would interpret it in such a way that the distinction between mud and pot is explained in terms of a cause-effect series (*hetu-phala-santāna*). This way is not open to the Sāṅkhya thinker. The transformation according to him implies oneness between cause and effect.

(25.4) 'उभयथा येन परिणामः' This reading is not satisfactory. Perhaps 'तस्मादुभयथापि न परिणामः' is the correct reading here because Śāntarakṣita says - 'तस्मादुभयथापि न परिणामः इत्युपसंहारः' (That is, Dharmakīrti sums up by saying - Therefore there is no transformation in both the cases).

(26.1) Here Viveka (= differentiation) probably means 'qualification' which differentiates one thing from its transformation. *Nirviveka* = unqualified.

(26.2) Sāṅkhya thinkers hold that a subtle (or non-manifest) object is not directly apprehended though it exists. (*Saukṣmyāt tadanupalabdhiḥ* - *Sāṅkhyakārikā,* verse 8.) A fist is non-manifestly existent in the fingers; hence it is not apprehended.

(26.3) The reading 'द्रव्यमेव निर्विवेकम् अवस्था' is not clear enough. My translation follows Śāntarakṣita's interpretation. "तत्त्वान्यत्वाभ्यामनिर्वचनीयं तदुक्तमिति वाक्यार्थः।"

(27.1) According to Sāṅkhya every effect is made up of three *guṇas* (strands) - *Sattva, Rajas* and *Tamas.* So every effect (product, manifestation) is pre-existent in the form of three *guṇas* according to them. And the cause already consists of three *guṇas.* So the Sāṅkhya thinker, who accepts pre-existence of all effects in their causes in the from of three *guṇas* will have to accept that anything can be produced from anything.

(27.2) Śāntarakṣita here refers to an argument - 'सतो यदि भवेज्जन्म, जातस्यापि भवेद् भवः' (The source is unknown) 'If generation of an existing thing is accepted, then a born thing can be born (again, i.e. without getting destroyed). The reading 'निःस्वभावावस्थायामिव' suggests that Dharmakīrti might be following Mādhyamikas here. But Śāntarakṣita refers to निष्पन्नावस्थायाम् as the reading, which removes this feeling.

(29.1) We can say that by introducing the notion of *Svabhāvānupalabdhi* Dharmakīrti is reducing difference to 'mutual non-existence' (*Anyonyābhāva* in Nyāya terminology), a kind of absence. He would say that 'pleasure is different from pain' means 'pleasure is non-existent in the form of pain'. And we can talk of this kind of absence because we can say, "If pleasure would have existed as pain, then it would have been apprehended in the form of pain. But it is not so apprehended. So pleasure does not exist as pain. That is, it is different from pain."

(29.2) 'उपदर्श्यानुपलब्धिनिर्देशाद मर्थनं स्वभावानुपलब्धौ' This part of the statement seems to be corrupt. Perhaps this was a part of some commentary, but projected into the text by some copy-writer. Any way, this statement-part has not been commented upon by Śāntarakṣita.

(31.1) 'कथं न प्रतिज्ञासाधनादयः' does not make a good sense. I have accepted 'कथं न प्रतिज्ञा साधनावयवः'. The same reading seems to have been accepted by Śāntarakṣita when he says - 'साधनावयवः प्रतिज्ञां प्राप्नोति' etc. in his commentary.

(31.2) Here the available reading of Dharmakīrti's argument does not seem to be clear and satisfactory.

(33.1) Here the reading seems to be corrupt and incomplete. The translation is tentative.

(33.2) Literally - ..... of the savants approved by good persons.

(34.1) That is, he can give another performance which cannot be repeated by the disputant and hence the disputant gets defeated.

(34.2) That is to say, bringing irrelevant topics in the course of debate is as irrelevant and improper as offering gifts and beating with a rod for proving one's point.

(35.1) According to the doctrine of *Pratītyasamutpāda* all products (*saṁskāras*) are dependent on many conditions (*pratyayas*). *Pratyayas* are of four kinds: *Hetu*, *Ālambana*, *Anantara* and *Adhipati*. Out of them *Hetu* is the cause (*Nirvartaka:* the sufficient condition) (See *Madhyamakaśāstra* 1.4. with *Prasannapadā*) Every composite object or a product is dependent on the cause and other conditions. This dependent or conditioned character of everything is necessarily linked up with its unpleasant character and also with its impermanence.

(35.2) 'प्रतिवादिनोजिज्ञासितस्य' can be read as 'प्रतिवादिनोऽजिज्ञासितस्य', i.e. 'प्रतिवादिनः अजिज्ञासितस्य' as I have done. If we accept 'जिज्ञासितस्य' as the reading, then the statement would imply that stating what is enquired by the opponent too is an occasion of defeat. But this would be inconsistent with another statement by Dharmakīrti - 'जिज्ञासायाम् अदोषः' (= If there is an enquiry then there is no fault.) (See section 33). The point is, even if a characteristic is relevant, it should not be expressed separately if it necessarily follows from the argument, except when there is an enquiry about that characteristic from the side of the opponent.

(35.3) If the disputant's argument is faulty, but the opponent does not point out the fault then neither does the disputant win (because his argument is faulty) nor does the opponent win (because he fails to discover the fault). This is prima facie inconsistent with *adoṣodbhāvana* (rather its first kind which will be explained in section 36) as an occasion of the opponent's defeat. For a discussion of this problem see the Introduction.

(36.1) Śāntarakṣita interprets. 'यत्र विषये' as 'जिज्ञासिते विषये' (That is, the object that is enquired). That is to say, the non-discovery of fault in the statement/argument regarding un-enquired object is not an occasion of defeat.

(36.2) I prefer *tat* to *tataḥ* which was accepted by Rahul Sankritryayana and makes better sense. Here *tat* refers to the occurrence of *adoṣodbhāvana.*

(37.1) The words पंसन and विपंसन are found in *R.* In Monier Monier-William's Sanskrit-English Dictionary the word पंसन is given along with the comment that it is probably a wrong reading for पांसन. The meaning of 'पांसन' is given as defiling, vitiating, disgracing, spoiling. The word विपांसन is not given in the Dictionary but it probably means the same as पंसन or पांसन.

(37.2) Śāntarakṣita adds - यश्छलादिभि: क्रियते इति अध्याहार:। He implies that the debate between the two debaters desirous of victory involves the use of quibbling etc., according to Naiyāyikas. Such a debate is not legitimate (= *yogavihita, nyāyya*) according to Dharmakīrti. Śāntarakṣita's interpretation also implies that Dharmakīrti was not critical about any debate between debaters desirous of victory but only if it involved quibbling and other practices of cheating. In fact Dharmakīrti seems to be revising the Nyāya concepts of victory and defeat to make them more conducive to academic spirit instead of getting rid of them completely.

(37.3) The point is this - The disputant should follow the norms of logic while arguing his position. The intention behind it should be to enlighten the opponent or to pervade him rationally and not to mislead or confuse him. If the opponent follows the argument advanced by the disputant, well and good. But if he does not follow it, the disputant should not try to confuse him or the audience by way of quibbling and other cheating practices. The purpose behind participation in debate should not be to cause non-apprehension or misapprehension (i.e. *apratipatti* or *vipratipatti*) but to remore them and avoid their arisal.

(38.1) *Jātis* are pseudo-refutations which are generally counter-arguments based on analogy. *Sādharmyasama* is a counter-argument based on positive analogy, *Vaidharmyasama* is the one based on negative analogy. A list of twenty four such *jātis* is given in *NS* for my discussion of which see my *Inference and Fallacies discussed in Ancient India Logic* (published by Indian Books Centre), Chapter VII, Part II.

(38.2) '... तत्त्वाप्रख्यापनात् अदोषोद्भावनं च' - The available reading is not satisfactory. The translation is tentative.

(39.1) Dharmakīrti, from this section onwards, critically discusses the 22 Nyāya-nigrahasthānas as they are defined and explained by Gautama, Vātsyāyana and Udyotakara. While responding to each Nyāya-nigrahasthāna he first quotes the Nyāya-aphorism, then some selected portions from the commentaries by Vātsyāyana and Udyotakara (Nyāyabhāṣya and Nyāyavārtika respectively) and then gives his response. But while quoting Nyāya position he does not always make it clear as to which commentary he is quoting. It may also be noted that Dharmakīrti does not always quote the commentaries very accurately but he seems to cite an abridged and even rephrased version of them. Sometimes he makes a free combination of Nyāyabhāṣya and Nyāyavārtika and states it as the *Pūrvapakṣa*.

(41.1) Here I have accepted the available reading 'जात्या प्रतिपद्येतापि चेत्'. But I suspect that the original reading should have been 'जाड्यात् प्रतिपद्येतापि चेत्' which is more consistent with the answer given by Dharmakīrti.

(42.1) This 'Nyāya explanation' is a free combination of *Nyāyabhāṣya* 5.2.3. and *Nyāya-vārtika* 5.2.3.

(43.1) Here Dharmakīrti is referring to the Nyāya definition of *hetu* viz. उदाहरणसाधर्म्यात् साध्यसाधनं हेतुः। (*NS* 1.1.34).

(47.1) Here Dharmakīrti is referring to Udyotakara's statement. But the statement in *Nyāyavārtika* is different from the one referred to by Dharmakīrti. The original statement runs - 'परपक्षसिद्धेन गोत्वादिनाऽनैकान्तिकदेशनाद् विरोधः यः परपक्षसिद्धेन गोत्वादिना व्यभिचारयति तद् विरुद्धमुत्तरं वेदितव्यम्।' Here Udyotakara is referring to three different cases and including them in *Pratijñāvirodha.*

(i) विरुद्धम् उत्तरम् - (Contrary Reply) Example - Suppose a Vaiśeṣika is the disputant. He might argue - "Sound is impermanent because it is perceptible through sense-organs". And suppose a Buddhist is the opponent. He points out - "Your probans is inconclusive. Because, 'Universal' which is accepted by you, is perceptible but not impermanent according to you." Here the opponent (Buddhist) is accusing the disputant (Vaisesika) of Inconclusiveness (*Anaikāntikadeśanā*) and pointing out a counter-instance which the disputant will have to accept but the opponent himself does not accept. (Because Buddhists do not believe in the existence of universals i.e. *jātis*)

(ii) स्वपक्षानपेक्षं च ...... विरुद्धः। This case is similar to the case (i). Here Vaiśeṣika disputant makes the same argument irrespective of his own position. In this example there is no mention of the opponent.

(iii) उभयपक्षसम्प्रतिपन्नः अनैकान्तिकः। In the above two cases the counterinstance was acceptable to one party but not to the other. But if the counter-instance is accepted by both the parties, then the probans will be inconclusive.

Dharmakīrti understands the first case in a different way. In his presentation probably Buddhist is the disputant and Vaiśeṣika is the opponent. The Buddhist argues that sound is impermanent because knowable through senses and Vaiśeṣika produces 'Universals' as the counterinstance.

In this discussion Udyotakara has used the term *viruddha* in a broad sense and not in the strict sense of the *viruddha - hetvābhāsa.*

(48.1) In this argument the word 'यस्य' should be supplied. So the argument will be -

'यस्य रूपादिभ्योऽर्थान्तरस्यानुपलब्धिः तद् गुणव्यतिरिक्तम्। नोपलभ्यते च रूपादिभ्योऽर्थान्तरं द्रव्यम्। (तस्माद् द्रव्यं गुणव्यतिरिक्तम्)।'

(48.2) In *Nyāyabindu,* Dharmakīrti discusses the fallacy called *iṣṭavighātakṛt* in the case of which the probans proves the opposite of the *intended* probandum. This fallacy was acknowledged by Diṅnāga as a special type of *Viruddha.* But Dharmakīrti includes it in *Viruddha* in general.

(48.3) 'कुतश्चिद् विप्रकर्षिणाम्' - Remote in some respect (or - remote for some reason). For example Dharmakīrti himself talks of remoteness of three kinds in Sec. 9.

(49.1) This is an answer to a possible objection that a Naiyāyika could raise. The Nyaiyāyika's possible objection is - Buddhists also use many probans for proving one and the same probandum. Similarly there is nothing wrong in pointing out many faults in one and the same argument.

(49.2) Dharmakīrti distinguishes between *svalakṣaṇa* (a self-characterised particular) and *sāmānyalakṣaṇa* (universal). The meaning (connotation) of a word is universal in nature. A universal is not ontologically real. *Svalakṣaṇa* is ontologically real, but it is not the meaning of a word. The statement 'Self does not exist' does not mean to deny the meaning of the word 'self', but it means to deny the existence of any ontologically real entity called 'self.'

(51.1) This example is given for showing that an instance need not be given always in the form 'like so and so', but it could be given even in the ablative form (*pañcamī*) meaning 'because so and so.'

(51.2) Śāntarakṣita comments : साधनप्रयोगोत्प्रेक्षासूचकं वाक्यमेतत्, नत्विदं साधनवाक्यमित्यर्थः।

(51.3) Śātarakṣita refers to a verse of Yogācāra Buddhists -

पङ्केन युगपद् योगात् परमाणोः पतङ्गताम् ।

षण्णां समानदेशत्वात् पिण्डः स्यादणुमात्रकः ॥

Meaning: Since atoms of earth get conjoined with the mud (= A *tryaṇuka* of earth composed of six atoms?) at once, therefore since the atom has no dimensions, it will be united with all the atoms in the same point of space and hence the cluster of atoms will be of the size of an atom only.

(52.1) This case of contrariety is called 'contrariety of probans (to the Declaration) based on falsification of Declaration' by Dharmakīrti in section 50. The earlier type of contrarity was 'contrariety of Declaration and probans to the means of knowledge' as referred to by Dharṃakīrti in section 47.

(53.1) The idea is this: The contrariety between probans and Declaration may take form of two fallacies - Contrary probans and Unproved probans. It probans exists in the locus, then probandum does not exist there due to contrarity. If on the other hand probans does not exist in the locus, then it is a clear case of Unproved probans. In the example "Everything is discrete because terms denoting reals stand for collections" the 'Unproved probans' is apparent immediately, which is the cause of the occasion of defeat. Contrariety may be discovered later when it has no significance.

(54.1) See Section 46.

(54.2) Presumably it is the same argument as 'Everything is discrete because the term 'real' is applicable to an aggregate only'. See section 46.

(55.1) 'भण्डालेख्यन्यायेन' In Sanskrit literature we find the use of many popular maxims (*laukika-nyāya*) Nyāya in this sense is a maxim or principle expressed in the form of an allegory. I have called it 'allegorical principle' in the translation. *Bhaṇḍālekhya-nyāya* is not mentioned in any standard Glossary of *nyāyas.* But it could be explained in the light of Śāntarakṣita's interpretation as follows. A buffoon (*Bhaṇḍa*) draws amusing suggestive sketches (*ālekhya*) and thereby indicates different realistic pictures by playing a gimic. He may use the same sketch for indicating different pictures at different times. Udyotakara is playing a similar gimic according to Dharmakīrt. Though the definition of 'Contrary Declaration' (*Pratijñāvirodha*) primarily applies to contrariety between Declaration and probans, Udyotakara extends the scope of this *nigrahasthāna* to other kinds of contrariety, for example, the contrariety between Declaration and Instance. In doing this he plays the same gimic as is suggested by the term '*Bhaṇḍālekhyanyāya*' according to Dharmakīrti.

(55.2) Here Dharmakīrti means probandum by '*Pakṣīkṛtadharma*' and probans by '*pakṣadharma.*'

(55.3) The idea is this. A contrary instance is that where there is absence of probandum. If probans exists in the contrary instances exclusively, that is, only in contrary instances and not in any other instances, that is, in non-probandum-possessing instances only and not in probandum-possessing instances then we could say, "Here probans is pervaded by the absence of probandum." That makes it a case of contrary probans.

(55.4) The example is, (following Śāntarakṣita) - " Sound is impermanent, because it differs from experience to experience, like space, unlike pot." Here space is given as a positive instance but actually it is a 'contrary instance' (*viruddha-dṛṣṭānta*) in the sense that it does not possess probandum (impermanence). Here the probans does not exist in this 'contrary positive instance', but it exists in the opposite (i.e. non-contrary) instance. The non-contrary instance is that which possesses probandum. Here pot is the non-contrary instance and probans (i.e. the quality of differing from experience to experience) exists in it. In fact here the major part of the argument is not fallacious but instances are fallacious because what should have been given as positive instance is given as negative instance and vice versa.

(55.5) 'The Contrariety of Declaration to the instance' here means non-existence of the Declared property, that is the probandum, in the instance. Such a non-existence would be fallacious if it is in the positive instance, not if it is in the negative instance.

(56.1) According to Naiyāyikas (i) *Pratijñā* (ii) *Hetu* (iii) *Dṛṣṭānta* (iv) *Upanaya* and (v) Nigamana is the correct order of the elements in an argument, that is, an inference for others. So if probans and instance both are faulty, the fault in the probans will count first, and since the debater is defeated by the first fault, the fault in the instance, which counts later, will be superfluous.

(57.1) Here the argument under consideration is - "The sound is permanent because knowable through senses" (See the note 47.1) A Buddhist proposes this argument and a Vaiśeṣika or Mīmāṁsaka opposes it by pointing out that Universals like 'cowness' are knowable through senses, but permanent. So the knowability through senses has a variable relation with impermanence.

(57.2) The idea is this. If the disputant's argument is well established, then cowness cannot succeeded as counterinstance, whether 'cowness' exists or not and if the argument is Inconclusive, then it is Inconclusive whether cowness exists or not. So this kind of *Pratijñāvirodha*, if it *is* an occasion of defeat, is covered by the fallacy of probans viz. Inconclusiveness.

(59.1) I have suggested अनिगृहीत एव (i.e. अनिगृहीते एव) in place of अनिगृह त एव which does not make any consistent sense. However the meaning of the statement is not still very clear.

(60.1) Śāntarakṣita explains the qualified probans as 'एकप्रकृतिसमन्वयत्वे सति परिणामदर्शनात्'. (The reading 'परिणामदर्शनात्' seems to be corrupt. It should be 'परिमाणदर्शनात्') The translation follows this explanation.

(62.1) *Kapolavādita* seems to mean *Kapola-tāḍita* or *Kapolatāḍana.* Monier-Williams gives the meaning of the latter expression: Striking the cheeks (as a token of confession of fault).

(62.2) *Kakṣya* means upper garment. I have accepted this as the correct reading in place of *Kaṅkṣya.* The word *Kaṅkṣya* as used in the available text is not found in Monier William's Dictionary.

(63.1) 'पर्षत्प्रतिभासपरिकल्प्यार्हवचनात्' This reading seems to be corrupt, as Śāntarakṣita quotes it differently as, 'पर्षत्प्रज्ञामिति'.

(64.1) The sentence runs 'दश दाडिमानि, षडपूपाः, कुण्डमजाजिनं, पललपिण्डम्, अथ रौरुकमेतत्, कुमार्याः पाय्यं तस्याः पिताऽप्रतिशीनः।' (Free translation - Ten pomegranates, six cakes, bowl, skin of a goat, a lump of ground sesamum, now this is *Yajus* of the Ruruka-school, protection of a girl child, her father is not frozen).

(64.2) The word *Kila* (= 'they say') perhaps refers to Udyotakara's explanation - 'तत्र हि वर्णमात्रम्, इह तु पदान्यसम्बद्धानि' (*Nyāyavārtika* 5.2.10).

(65.1) 'पूर्वं कर्मोपादीयते ततः करणं मृत्पिण्डादिकं लोके।' Udyotakara seems to mean by this statement that the order of words is adjusted in accordance with meaning. The 'meaning' is the *karma* (= object) of action (viz., knowing). It is taken into account first. Then the words are apprehended in their proper order. Apprehension of words is the *Karaṇa* (instrument) of the knowledge of the sentence-meaning. [As Viśvanātha puts it in his *Kārikāvalī* - पदज्ञानं तु करणं ... शाब्दबोधः फलं तत्र ... ॥81॥]

(66.1) That an incorrect word conveys the meaning via the correct word, is originally the view referred to by Grammarians. (Bhartṛhari, for instance, refers to this view in *Vākyapadīya, Brahmakāṇḍa,* verses 147-155). The grammarian who holds this view is speaking non-sense according to Dharmakīrti. And Naiyāyika is another mad person (according to Dharmakīrti) who is narrating and using the faulty perspective of the grammarian. It is to be noted, however, that grammarian's position on the issue of corrupt words (*apabhraṁśas*) is rather complex. In *Vākyapadīya* 1.152 Bhartṛhari says that in certain cases the corrupt word conveys its meaning via the correct word. But in 1.53 he says that when corrupt words become customary among the speakers of lower starta (women, śūdras etc.), the corrupt words are directly meaningful, whereas the correct words fail to convey their meaning. Of course grammarians give some sanctity to 'correct' (*sādhu*) words. They attach some religious merit to them. Dharmakīrti rightly criticises this view.

(66.2) Since a very long time women and śūdras were not allowed to use the 'cultured' language (Sanskrit) of the Brahmins. Majority of them were quite ignorant about most of the so-called correct words. The words well-formed according to Paninian Grammar were supposed to be the correct words or the standard words (*sādhu-śabda*). Other words were non-standard words (*asādhu-śabda*). Non-standard words did not strictly belong to Sanskrit language. They could belong to the so-called Prakrit (= natural, vulgar?) language or Apabhraṁśa (corrupt) language.

(67.1) The reading 'नगपातम्' is likely to be corrupt. The meaning is not clear.

(67.2) The idea is this. Grammarians and Naiyāyikas following them attribute some special sanctity to Sanskrit words in virtue of their well-defined (i.e. grammatically well-formed) character (= *sādhutva*). This is the same as correctness or culturedness (Sanskritness) of these words, which is supposed to owe its status to the rules of Sanskrit grammar. This view is not acceptable to Dharmakīrti. According to him we judge 'correctness' or 'incorrectness' of them, not due to any well-defined or essential character of words but due to some other reason. The other reason is the tradition of word-usage at the hands of experienced persons. Śāntarakṣita calls it वृद्धप्रवादपारम्पर्य. And this cause of correctness is common to Sanskrit and non-Sanskrit language alike. So there is no special sanctity of Sanskrit language.

(67.3) The tendency to attribute a well-defined character to words is the tendency to attribute a fixed character to them independent of usage or convention.

(67.4) In 'सम्बन्धप्रतीतिर्न, न विपर्ययः' one 'न' is additional and may be omitted for the sake of consistent meaning.

(68.2) In fact the word to word translation of 'पुरुषो राज्ञः' would be 'Man king's' (when the actual meaning is 'King's man'). This translation is not permitted in English. But in Sanskrit such a reversal of words is allowed and makes a good sense without any oddity.

(68.3) In Sanskrit the order of words is generally unimportant. The semantical position of words is fixed by the suffixes attached to them and not by their syntactical order. In English the order of words generally plays a discisive role in fixation of meaning. For instance 'Cow bring the black' will either make no sense or at least will not make the same sense as 'Bring the black cow'. But 'गाम् आनय कृष्णाम्', 'कृष्णां गाम् आनय', 'आनय कृष्णां गाम्' all make the same sense in Sanskrit.

(68.4) According to Dharmakīrti the argument (i.e. the inference for others) consists of two steps: one indicates pervasion between probans and probandum and the other indicates existence of probans in the property-bearer (*dharmī*). The property-bearer is to be proved to be possessing probandum as its another property. These two steps could be presented in any order. Declaration or conclusion is not necessary as a step in the argument because they are entailed by the two steps mentioned above.

(69.1) This is a reference to Udyotakara according to Śāntarakṣita.

(71.1) In the five-membered inferential statement of *Nyāya*, Conclusion (= the last element) is the repetition of Declaration (= the first element). But this repetition is permitted by the author of *NS*, because it is *Anuvāda* (= a repetition which explains or confirms the earlier statement). The repetitions which are not confirmatory like this are not permitted.

(71.2) Here probably the metaphor of a machine is used for denoting a slave.

(71.3) Here the word *hasati* (= (1) laughs (2) when laughs), *dhāvati/pradhāvati* (= (1) runs (2) when runs), *nindati/praṇindati* (= (1) censures (2) when censures), *nṛtyati/pranṛtyati* (= (1) dances (2) when dances) are used twice but in two different senses.

(71.4) Here the word *bhavati* is used twice in two different senses ((1) happens (2) when (it) happens).

(72.1) This is a restatement of the Nyāya aphorism 'अर्थादापन्नस्य स्वशब्देन पुनर्वचनम्' (*NS* 5.2.15).

(72.2) According to Naiyāyikas an elaborate discussion which is not regulated by the rules of victory and defeat is permitted if it is between a teacher and disciple or between two co-disciples (See *NS* 4.2.48) but not between others. The debate between others should be regulated by the constraints of *nigrahasthānas*. It should not be diffuse and repetitive.

(73.1) The original reading is corrupt and confusing. I am following *V* in the translation. Śāntarakṣita too takes this statement as elliptical and adds - 'प्रपञ्चकथायाम् अदोषः इत्यभिसम्बन्धः।'

(73.2) Dharmakīrti has said this in sections 62 and 64.

(73.3) Here my translation follows Śāntarakṣita's commentary. He takes 'अर्थः पुनः प्रतिपादनात् न भिद्यते' to mean 'अर्थपुनरुक्तं हेतूदाहरणाधिकात् न भिद्यते'.

(79.1) I suggest 'अप्रतिभयैव' in place of 'अत्रेति तत्रैव' the latter being not sufficiently clear. But I have translated following the available reading somehow.

(79.2) That is, either *Ajñāna* is an occasion of defeat via *Apratibhā* or *Ajñāna* is not an (independent) occasion of defeat at all because its scope is pervaded by *Apratibhā*. Here I have suggested 'अप्रतिभाया' in place of 'अप्रतिभया' as an alternative reading, the former being consistent with later discussion. (See the last sentence of the same section)

(80.1) 'निग्रहस्थानान्तराणि वाच्यानि' will be grammatically more correct and semantically consistent, than 'निग्रहस्थानान्तरालवाच्यानि'. But the word 'अन्तराल' might be there in the original text which might refer to 'intermediate' occasions of defeat. By incorporating it an alternative reading may be suggested - 'अन्तरालनिग्रहस्थानान्तराणि वाच्यानि।'

(80.2) The other such sub-divisions would be 'not understanding the half of the answer', 'not understanding one third of the answer', similarly, 'not understanding the whole subject-matter', 'not understanding the half of the subject-matter' etc.

(82.1) This Nyāya-explanation as quoted by Dharmakīrti here is a free combination of *Nyāyabhāṣya* and *Nyāyavārtika* on *NS* 5.2.20.

(83.1) In other words, whether it is an argument presented by the disputant or the response given by the opponent, it is regulated by the two-fold negative check: Fallacies of probans and Non-imagination.

(83.2) *Vitaṇḍā* means the kind of debate where the debaters present no position of their own, but they only try to refute the other debater's position.

(84.1) Naiyāyika's objection is this: You have said that all the occasions of defeat committed by the disputant could be included in *Hetvābhāsa* and all the occasions of defeat committed by the opponent could be included in *Apratibhā*. But we are now citing a case which is an occasion of defeat

Glossary

of technical terms used in *Vādanyāya*

अज्ञान (– निग्रहस्थान) - Non-understanding

अतिप्रसङ्ग - transgression (of reason)

अतिशय - excess

अदोषोद्भावन - (1) Not pointing out a fault (2) Pointing out a non-fault as fault.

अधिक (– निग्रहस्थान) - Additional

अननुभाषण (– निग्रहस्थान) - Non-reproduction

अनन्वय (–दृष्टान्ताभास) - Positive instance without positive concomitance

अनवस्थाप्रसङ्ग - Occurrence of (vicious) infinite regress.

अनुपलब्धि - non-apprehension

अनुपलम्भ - non-apprehension

अनुवाद - confirmatory repetition

अनैकान्तिक (– हेत्वाभास) - Inconclusive probans

अनैकान्तिकचोदना - accusation of Inconclusive probans

अन्वय - (1) positive concomitance (2) continuity, continuous capasity

अपशब्द - incorrect word, corrupt word

अपसिद्धान्त (– निग्रहस्थान) - Deviant thesis

अपार्थक (– निग्रहस्थान) - Non-sensical

अप्रतिपत्ति - non-apprehension, non-understanding

अप्रतिभा (– निग्रहस्थान) - Non-imagination

अप्रदर्शितान्वय (– दृष्टान्ताभास) - Positive instance without the indication of positive concomitance

अप्राप्तकाल (– निग्रहस्थान) - Mistimed

अर्थक्रिया - function, pragmatic function

अर्थपुनरुक्त - Repetition of meaning

अर्थान्तर (– निग्रहस्थान) - Different point

अर्थान्तरगमन - Shifting to a Different point

अवयव - element (of argument), step (in argument)

अवयवान्तरवादिन् - the one who claims that instance is a different element of proof from probans

अवयविन् - composite whole

अवस्था - state

असद्व्यवहार - the linguistic practice of non-existence, the practice of non-existence

असाधनाङ्गवचन - (1) non-statement or non-justification of a constituent of proof (2) statement of a non-constituent of proof.

असिद्ध (– हेत्वाभास) - Unproved probans

असिद्धि - unprovedness

उपनय - Application (of instance to the thesis-case)

उपलब्धिलक्षणप्राप्त - apprehensible, (the object) fulfilling the condition of apprehensibility.

कार्यहेतु - effect as reason

छल - (1) quibbling (2) cheating

त्रिरूप हेतु - probans with triple character (1. existence in thesis-case, 2. existence in similar cases, 3. non-existence in dissimilar cases)

दूषण - (1) refutation, (2) fault

दृष्टान्ताभास - fallacy of instance

धर्मिन् - property-bearer

नान्तरीयकता - invariable relation

निगमन -Conclusion

निग्रहस्थान - occasion of defeat

निरनुयोज्यानुयोग (– निग्रहस्थान) - Objecting against the non-objectionable

निरर्थक (– निग्रहस्थान) - Meaningless utterance

न्याय - (1) logic (2) rationality (3) an allegorical principle

न्यून - Insufficient, Deficient

न्यूनत्व - Deficiency

पक्ष - (1) subject of the thesis, property-bearer, (2) position

पक्षधर्मवचन - the statement that the probans characterises the thesis-subject.

परिणाम - transformation

पर्यनुयोज्योपेक्षण (– निग्रहस्थान) - Neglecting the objectionable

पर्षत् - audience, assembly, council

पुनरुक्त (– निग्रहस्थान) - Repetition

पूर्वपक्षवादी - proposer of the first position

प्रकृति - Nature, original nature

प्रतिज्ञा - Declaration

प्रतिज्ञान्तर (– निग्रहस्थान) - Another Declaration

प्रतिज्ञाविरोध (– निग्रहस्थान) - Contrary Declaration, (Lit.-) Contrariety of/to Declaration.

प्रतिज्ञासंन्यास (– निग्रहस्थान) - Renunciation of Declaration

प्रतिज्ञाहानि (– निग्रहस्थान) - Declaration-abandonment

प्रतिवादिन् - opponent, respondent

प्रपञ्चकथा - diffuse discussion

प्रमाण - evidence, means to knowledge

प्रमेय - object of knowledge

प्रसङ्ग - (1) occasion, context, (2) undesirable consequence

भण्डालेख्यन्याय - the allegorical principle viz. (one plays a gimic) like the picture drawn by a buffoon

मतानुज्ञा (– निग्रहस्थान) - Permitting opponent's view.

लाघव - economy, (Lit.-) lightness

लिङ्ग - inferential sign, probans, reason

वाद - debate (Dharmakīrti), discussion between teacher and disciple or co-disciples for knowing truth (Nyāya)

वादिन् - disputant, proposer (of the first position)

विक्षेप (– निग्रहस्थान) - Dispensation

विजिगीषुवाद - debate between persons desiring victory (even by cheating practices)

वितण्डा - negative debate (debate in which the other's position is confuted without establishing one's own)

विप्रतिपत्ति - non-apprehension, non-understanding

विरुद्ध - contrary, contradictory

विरुद्ध (– हेत्वाभास) - Contrary probans

विरोध - contrariety, contradiction

विषय - subject-matter, object

विस्तरकथा - diffuse discussion

वैधर्म्यवत् प्रयोग - argument containing dissimilarity (i.e. negative concomitance)

व्यक्त - the Manifest (Sāṅkhya)

व्यतिरेक - negative concomitance, absence

व्यभिचार - variable relation

व्यापक - pervader

व्याप्त - pervaded

व्याप्ति - pervasion

व्याप्यं - pervaded

शक्ति - capasity

शब्दपुनरुक्त - Repetition of words

सद्व्यवहार - the practice/linguistic practice of existence

समय - convention

समर्थन - justification

साधन - (1) argument, proof (2) probans

साधनवाक्य - inferential statement, argument

साधनाभास - fallacy of argument/probans

साधनावयव - element of argument, step in argument

साधर्म्यवत् प्रयोग - argument containing (the statement of) similarity (i.e. positive concomitance)

साध्य - probandum, provable

साध्यविकल (- दृष्टान्ताभास) - Positive instance lacking probandum